little books for

BUSY MOMS

Planes, Trains, & Automobiles ... With Kids!

Resources from MOPS

Books

Beyond Macaroni and Cheese
A Cure for the Growly Bugs and Other Tips for Moms
Getting Out of Your Kids' Faces and Into Their Hearts
Loving and Letting Go
Mom to Mom
Meditations for Mothers
A Mother's Footprints of Faith
Ready for Kindergarten
What Every Child Needs
What Every Mom Needs
When Husband and Wife Become Mom and Dad
Little Books for Busy Moms
    Boredom Busters
    Great Books to Read and Fun Things to Do with Them
    If You Ever Needed Friends, It's Now
    Juggling Tasks, Tots, and Time
    Kids' Stuff and What to Do with It
    Planes, Trains, and Automobiles . . . with Kids!
    Time Out for Mom . . . Ahhh Moments

Books with Drs. Henry Cloud and John Townsend

Raising Great Kids
Raising Great Kids for Parents of Preschoolers Workbook
Raising Great Kids for Parents of Teenagers Workbook
Raising Great Kids for Parents of School-Age Children Workbook

Gift Books

God's Words of Life from the Mom's Devotional Bible
Mommy, I Love You Just Because

Kids Books

Little Jesus, Little Me
My Busy, Busy Day
See the Country, See the City
Mommy, May I Hug the Fishes?
Mad Maddie Maxwell
Zachary's Zoo
Morning, Mr. Ted
Boxes, Boxes Everywhere
Snug as a Bug?

Bible

Mom's Devotional Bible

Audio

Raising Great Kids

Curriculum

Raising Great Kids for Parents of Preschoolers *Zondervan*Groupware™
(with Drs. Henry Cloud and John Townsend)

little books for

BUSY MOMS

Planes, Trains,
& Automobiles ...
With Kids!

MOTHERS OF
M♥PS.
PRESCHOOLERS
...because mothering matters

MARY BETH LAGERBORG general editor
written by CYNTHIA W. SUMNER

ZONDERVAN™

GRAND RAPIDS, MICHIGAN 49530

ZONDERVAN™

Planes, Trains, and Automobiles ... with Kids!
Copyright © 2001 by Cynthia W. Sumner

Requests for information should be addressed to:
Zondervan, *Grand Rapids, Michigan 49530*

Library of Congress Cataloging-in-Publication Data

Sumner, Cynthia W.
    Planes, trains, and automobiles—with kids! / Mary Beth
Lagerborg, general editor; written by Cynthia W. Sumner.
        p. cm. — (Little books for busy moms)
      ISBN 0-310-23999-0
      1. Travel.   2. Children—Travel.   3. Family recreation.
I. Lagerborg, Mary Beth.   II. Title.   III. Series.
G151 . S86 2001
910'.2'02083—dc21   2001026748

Published in association with the literary agency of Alive Communications, Inc., 7680 Goddard Street, Suite 200, Colorado Springs, CO 80920.

Interior design by Melissa Elenbaas

Printed in the United States of America

01 02 03 04 05 /❖ DC/ 10 9 8 7 6 5 4 3 2 1

To my parents,
who first showed me
this wide and wonderful world

Contents

Help for Busy Moms

WHAT IMAGE DOES THE PHRASE "family vacation" call to mind? Immediately I am transported to family trips across sweltering Kansas in August to reach the cool mountain oasis of Colorado. My dad drove a big Oldsmobile in those days before air-conditioning. A thick, padded armrest pulled down from the center of the backseat. My older brother laid his head on the armrest and stuck his bare feet out one open window, while I laid with my head on the same headrest with my toes out the other window (imagine the potential for arguments when heads bumped together!). Coloring books and small toys blew around chaotically in the back window.

Up front, my younger brother, who was regularly afflicted with car sickness, sat between my parents. No wonder my father kept his foot to the pedal to make the miles go quicker. We never stopped to see the local sights: the World's Largest Ball of Twine, the Five-Legged Calf, the World's Largest Groundhog, or even the Tower Where You Can See Six States.

Those car trips hold fond memories for me—although I wish we'd stopped to see the sights! But I can just imagine the headache they were for my mom.

Here you are, Mom, faced with far more than planning a family outing or vacation. Before you is the opportunity to raise adventurers who are curious and confident in exploring their world. You can compile a rich store of family experiences, inside jokes, and even misery that you all will laugh about for years to come.

Traveling with kids takes planning and lots of savvy. It takes clinging to the big picture of expectations when car trouble or whining sets in. And it takes the willingness to be an adventurer yourself!

Author and mom Cynthia Sumner draws on a lifetime of family wanderlust to give you the tools and tips you'll need, plus the attitude that will almost guarantee family fun no matter where you roam.

At MOPS International (Mothers of Preschoolers) we believe that better moms make a better world. To be the best they can be, moms solicit advice from parenting experts and family members. But sometimes the best help of all comes from other moms who, traveling the same road, have made some great discoveries they're willing to pass along. Thus the series Little Books for Busy Moms was born. We've chosen topics to meet the needs of moms, presented in a format you can read quickly and easily. Like this one. We hope you use *Planes, Trains, and Automobiles...with Kids!* to help make family travel the great adventure it can be.

MARY BETH LAGERBORG
PUBLISHING MANAGER,
MOPS INTERNATIONAL
(MOTHERS OF PRESCHOOLERS)

Personally Speaking

A LOVE OF TRAVEL comes naturally to me. My parents devoted a large portion of their disposable income each year to visiting new places, always with my sister and me in tow. Thanks to their wanderlust I've visited thirty-seven of the fifty United States and many foreign countries as well.

Whether it was our annual summer vacation trip or one of our weekend jaunts to another city or state, my mother made traveling as a family look easy. That's not to say we didn't have our share of mishaps: my sister at age four locking herself in the airplane bathroom; unexpected visits to uninhabited (and uninhabitable) parts of major cities; a moose eating my sandwich through the car window. But generally our trips went very smoothly.

Later, as a mother of young children, when the walls of our apartment began to close in on me, I did what came naturally. I started planning a trip. It was then that I quickly discovered the truth: Traveling with kids is *not* easy! All the planning and preparation that had made those trips with my parents seem so effortless had somehow escaped my attention as a child. Simply piling into the car and hoping to find a place to stay along the way was not a viable vacation plan for a family with three young children. But for my husband and me, traveling to different places was too integral a part of our lives to give it up.

Over the years we have traveled by plane, train, and automobile with our children, including a thousand-mile trek each year to visit my extended family. Each first trip using a different mode of transportation has been a rite of initiation, but with each subsequent journey we have learned more of what to do to enjoy traveling together (and often more important, what *not* to do).

When I mentioned to friends that I was writing a book on traveling with children, their overwhelming response was to laugh and say, "Just don't do it!" Admittedly, trips with kids are not for the faint of heart. However, my travel experiences have shown and taught me things I would, in turn, like to pass on to my own children. In the United States alone there is an astounding level of diversity in scenery, local customs, food specialties, and even speech patterns.

Our kids delight in the family's annual trip to the Gulf Coast after living the rest of the year in the landlocked Midwest. Conversely, visitors to our home love to wander through the whispering rows of summer corn. As the scope of their world grows, kids become more open to new experiences and ideas. They also gain perspective about their place in the larger world around them.

Family travel brings something more to parents too: an appreciation of simple pleasures along the way. Because they have no personal agenda to follow, kids notice the smaller and often more delightful sights that adults may pass over. On our most recent trip my children discovered beach glass, lichen in three different colors, and hummingbirds visiting a lodge porch. (I learned that a hotel swimming pool can be a vacation destination!)

One of my favorite parts of the Bible is in chapter one of the book of Genesis. The author repeatedly uses the phrase "And God saw that it was good" after describing various stages of the creation of earth and everything in it. Wow! If God feels that way, then his world is something I want to see too. But beyond enjoying the wonders of God's creation, my best answer to "Why would you travel with kids?" would have to be because it brings a family closer together. Family vacation memories are among the few where adversity is remembered as fondly as comfort. We recall with equal affinity the beautiful lodge-hotel where we stayed at Walt Disney World and the leaky tent on another trip that drove us to invade the grandparents' screened-in cabin.

Will traveling with kids limit the choices for your itinerary? Maybe. Will the fact that your children accompany you make the trip more stressful? Probably. But will the journey together lead to a richer experience for everyone? Most certainly. In writing this book, my wish for those who have not yet embarked on such an adventure with children is that you will gain the confidence to venture away from the security of home, and that the information presented here will equip all parents with the information they need to plan and execute a trip that all family members can enjoy, not just endure. Happy trails to you!

Acknowledgments

IT HAS BEEN A PRIVILEGE to write a book about a subject so close to my heart, one that has brought me enjoyment throughout my life. I am most grateful to my parents, as well as to my grandparents, who always set such positive examples by inviting me to accompany them on their travels.

Thank you also:

To my husband, John, and my children, who love going new places as much as I do and are willing to brave the uncertainties of travel.

To my sister Cheryl, who has generously used her vacation time to go with us on trips when we're "roughing it."

To all of my friends at MOPS, especially my editor, Mary Beth Lagerborg, who have given me so many opportunities to stretch and grow and have cheered on my every step.

To the members of my book-discussion group, Tina Acree, Barbie Becker, Deanna Lustfeldt, Anne Zumwalt, Cheryl Geiger, Gwen McTaggart, and Kathy Orme, as well as my friends Lisa Gocken, Sally Allhands, and Dove Wong, who support my endeavors with their kind words and their own experiences.

To Joan Cook, whose information and expertise make this book complete and who has helped arrange wonderful trips for our family.

To my editor, Sandy Vander Zicht, who inspires me in many different ways to become a better writer.

To my agent, Chip MacGregor, for helping my voice to be heard.

To all my fellow travelers who kindly share the tips and insights that make our journeys more interesting and more comfortable.

choosing Where to Go

DECIDING WHERE TO GO on a trip is like filling up a plate for you and your child at a cafeteria buffet. You may love shrimp but feel it is too expensive and choose chicken instead. Even though you love broccoli, your child doesn't, so you compromise with green beans.

Likewise, when you sit down in front of a blank pad of paper to plan your travels, the world is your smorgasbord. It may be that your travel options are wide open. Or perhaps, like our family, you have friends and relatives to visit during vacation. And in addition to your ultimate destination there are also choices to make regarding which route to take, what to stop and see along the way, and what to do during your stay.

DISCUSS EXPECTATIONS

If this is your maiden vacation as a family, the first step in selecting a destination is to adjust your expectation of what a "vacation" means from before you had kids. A friend of mine and her husband once had the opportunity to go away for a romantic weekend at a resort. Her mother offered to care for their three-month-old son, but my friend declined, feeling she wasn't ready to be separated from her infant. In her words, "It was a disaster! Now it's even harder for us to get away alone, and I wish I had that weekend back to do over." She learned the hard way that unscheduled time for relaxation and intimacy is not usually compatible with a family trip.

Whenever you travel, all adults who will be going along should frankly discuss their goals for the trip and consider how best to accomplish them. Do you want to relax? See new sites? Commune with nature? Children who can articulate what they enjoy doing should be invited to join the discussion too. Defining your family's travel "likes" and "dislikes" naturally narrows the choice of locales.

CONSIDER AGES AND STAGES

Choosing where to go on a trip with an eye toward entertaining your child can make a trip a more positive experience for everyone. Kids may find certain destinations more appealing depending on their age and developmental stage in life. Taking these factors into account can help further define your list of destinations.

Infants

Until the time they begin to walk, most babies' motto is "I only want to be with you." As long as a trip accommodates their schedule, babies will go anywhere. If you bring along a stroller or front baby carrier, your infant can travel in comfort. When our first son was seven months old, we accompanied my husband on a business trip to Washington, D.C., over a long weekend. We walked everywhere, around monuments and through museums. It was the easiest trip we ever took! Our son was happy to enjoy the sights with us while riding high in a backpack carrier.

Toddlers and Preschoolers

Children in this age group usually do not enjoy sitting for long periods of time. They want to be on the move. Select destinations with several attractions located nearby to keep additional travel time to a minimum. Visit a city with a children's museum (they usually have exhibits for kids of all ages) and a zoo, along with other attractions; or stay in a beach house or condo with a water park and aquarium in the vicinity.

Any place with hands-on activities and room to run around unhindered will please your toddler or pre-schooler. And don't forget to build rest times or quiet activities into your day to avoid behavioral meltdowns!

School-Age Kids

Catering to a child's specific interests at this age will win you big points in terms of cooperation and happy family memories. Tours, museums, theme parks, or other venues specializing in sports, science, art, and different cultures encourage a child's passion and allow you to share that passion at the same time. More physically demanding outdoor trips are appropriate depending on strength and endurance levels (theirs and yours).

Teenagers

Traveling with teenagers affords you the most latitude in choosing a place to go, provided you can work around their busy schedules. Teens may acquiesce to a sightseeing excursion (as long as the sight is spectacular). Historical sites, adventure vacations, and more extensive traveling tours are possible.

Children's Museums

The popularity of children's museums is growing by leaps and bounds, as evidenced by the fact that several metropolitan areas like Los Angeles and Miami are in the process of building large new facilities. However, city tourism offices often neglect to include information about these special attractions in packets sent to inquiring visitors. Here is a list of children's museums in prominent cities across the country.

Austin, TX
Austin Children's Museum
201 Colorado Street
Austin, TX 78701
(512) 472-2499
www.austinkids.org

Berkeley, CA
Habitot Children's Museum
2065 Kittredge Street
Berkeley, CA 94704
(510) 647-1111
www.habitot.org

Boston, MA
The Children's Museum
300 Congress Street
Boston, MA 02210
(617) 426-8855
www.bostonkids.org

Brooklyn, NY
Brooklyn Children's Museum
145 Brooklyn Avenue
Brooklyn, NY 11213
(718) 735-4400
www.fieldtrip.com/ny/87354
400.htm

Chicago, IL
Chicago Children's Museum
700 East Grand Avenue at
    Navy Pier
Chicago, IL 60611
(312) 527-1000
www.chichildrensmuseum.org

Cincinnati, OH
Cinergy Children's Museum
1301 Western Avenue
Cincinnati, OH 45203
(513) 287-7000
www.cincymuseum.org/3mus
    eums/childrens.asp

Denver, CO
The Children's Museum of
    Denver
2121 Children's Museum
    Drive
Denver, CO 80211
(303) 433-7444
www.cmdenver.org

Houston, TX
The Children's Museum of
    Houston

1500 Binz
Houston, TX 77004
(713) 522-1138
www.cmhouston.org

Indianapolis, IN
The Children's Museum of
   Indianapolis
3000 N. Meridian Street
Indianapolis, IN 46208
(317) 924-KIDS
www.childrensmuseum.org

Las Vegas, NV
Lied Discovery Children's
   Museum
833 Las Vegas Blvd. N
Las Vegas, NV 89101
(702) 382-3445
www.ldcm.org

Memphis, TN
The Children's Museum of
   Memphis
2525 Central Avenue
Memphis, TN 38104
(901) 458-2678
www.cmom.com

New Orleans, LA
Louisiana Children's Museum
420 Julia Street
New Orleans, LA 70130
(504) 523-1357
www.lcm.org

New York, NY
Children's Museum of Man-
   hattan
The Tisch Building

212 W. 83rd Street
New York, NY 10024
(212) 721-1234
www.cmom.org

Pittsburgh, PA
The Pittsburgh Children's
   Museum
10 Children's Way
Pittsburgh, PA 15212
(412) 322-5058
www.pittsburghkids.org

Portland, OR
Children's Museum
4015 SW Canyon Road
Portland, OR 97221
(503) 823-2227
www.pdxchildrensmuseum.org

St. Louis, MO
The Magic House
516 S. Kirkwood Road
St. Louis, MO 63122
(314) 822-8900
www.magichouse.com

St. Paul, MN
Minnesota Children's
   Museum
10 West Seventh Street
St. Paul, MN 55102
(651) 225-6001
www.mcm.org

Salt Lake City, UT
Children's Museum of Utah
840 N 300 West
Salt Lake City, UT 84103
(801) 322-5268
www.childmuseum.org

Seattle, WA
The Children's Museum
305 Harrison Street

Seattle, WA 98109
(206) 441-1768
www.thechildrensmuseum.org

Washington, D.C.
Capital Children's Museum
800 3rd St. NE
Washington, D.C. 20002
(202) 675-4120
www.ccm.org

CHOOSE A DESTINATION

Once you have a handle on your family's expectations for the trip, the next step is to decide where you'll be going. I try to have some destination ideas on hand by keeping a "vacation" file. Anytime I read an article in the "Travel" section of the newspaper or in a magazine that features a place I think we'd like to visit, I clip it out and put it in a file. You can even expand one file into a system, with a file for your particular state, one for nearby regional areas, and a file for the state where you visit your relatives.

By far the best recommendation for a travel destination will come from another family who has already been there. Have you noticed that travel brochures and articles *always* make a place seem more beautiful and exciting than the real thing? As with any major purchase the lesson is "Let the buyer beware." Friends who have actually visited a location can give you the straight scoop on the quality of accommodations and the quantity of activities available. Just remember that another family's likes and dislikes may differ from yours, which means their idea of a good time and yours may not be compatible.

CONSULT A TRAVEL AGENT

Another good resource for choosing where to go is your local travel agency. Beyond the glossy brochures, a travel agent hears about clients' successes and failures. An agent with a family may have traveled extensively and be willing to share their experiences.

In addition to experience there are several other reasons to make use of a travel agent's services. Agencies have easy access to travel information, which will save you time doing research and making reservations. An agent may also be able to save you money with travel packages and promotions.

If you run into problems on a trip, a travel agent can run interference and offer assistance. And for those planning to embark on a tour or other vacation package, a travel agent can arrange trip cancellation insurance, which refunds the cost of the trip if you must bow out due to illness or injury of a family member.

How should you select a travel agent? According to my friend (and travel agent) Joan Cook, the number one consideration should be choosing someone with a lot of experience, both as an agent and a traveler. Ask your friends for recommendations if you're not sure where to begin.

OTHER CONSIDERATIONS

We always take two additional factors into account before making a final decision: variety and flexibility. If we reserve a house on the lake for a week, will our vacation be blown if it rains for three days straight? A good choice of location insures a good time no matter what Mother Nature throws your way. One year, during our annual week at the beach, we had a rain out. Luckily, the city of Galveston was nearby, so we took advantage of several of its indoor attractions: a train museum, an old-fashioned ice cream parlor, a rain forest habitat, a million-gallon aquarium, and seashell shops.

I know that someday our children will tire of the beach, but for now they enjoy our summer tradition. We keep our trips fresh by seeing different sights while there and by taking different routes to and from Texas each time. For example, two years ago we visited New Orleans and Mammoth Cave; last year we stayed in a cabin in Arkansas and toured St. Louis.

If you are unsure how your child will react to a vacation activity, do a trial run *before* you go. See how he responds to a museum trip, a visit to the beach, or a hike in the woods. In choosing where to go, bear in mind that there is no "perfect" family vacation spot. Regardless of your destination, thoughtful preparation improves the likelihood that the trip will be an enjoyable one for all.

Planning Ahead

AS MOTHERS WE UNDERSTAND the importance of keeping things running smoothly with children along. Researching your travel destination and mode of transportation can be the most tedious aspect of preparing for a trip, yet it is also the step that yields the greatest rewards. By planning well in advance, families can save themselves time, money, and a lot of grief.

Thank goodness we live in the information age. For families, the more information they can gather before embarking on a trip, the better. In addition to traditional resources like maps and travel books, a wealth of information is now available via your telephone and home computer.

GET MORE INFORMATION

Although you've chosen your ultimate destination, you might like more information about other things nearby to see and do. Tourism is big business these days, so most cities and states encourage travel to their area by offering abundant free information on places and activities of interest.

States

Every state has a web site of its own that can be accessed by inserting the appropriate two-letter state abbreviation into the blanks in this general address: www.state.—.us

For example, the web address for my home state of Illinois is www.state.il.us. When you get to a state web site look for key words like *visit*, *travel*, and *tourism*. Clicking on these links will lead to pages containing information about various attractions and, in many cases, travel guides that can be ordered or downloaded directly to your computer.

For those not yet on-line, each state offers a toll-free number from which to order comparable information. States that aggressively pursue tourism dollars staff phone lines twenty-four hours a day so you can call at your convenience. As an added benefit to using the phone, many of these states have "travel consultants" available (a real, live person!) to

answer questions about a specific location. Be fore-
warned that some variation exists in the ease of use
and the amount of information available from both
state web sites and tourism offices.

Alabama (AL)	800-ALA-BAMA
Alaska (AK)	800-327-5774
Arizona (AZ)	800-842-8257
Arkansas (AR)	800-643-8383
California (CA)	800-TO-CALIF
Colorado (CO)	800-265-6723
Connecticut (CT)	800-CT-BOUND
Delaware (DE)	800-441-8846
Florida (FL)	888-7-FLAUSA
Georgia (GA)	800-VISIT-GA
Hawaii (HI)	800-GO-HAWAII
Idaho (ID)	800-VISIT-ID
Illinois (IL)	800-226-6632
Indiana (IN)	800-289-6646
Iowa (IA)	800-345-IOWA
Kansas (KS)	800-252-6727
Kentucky (KY)	800-225-TRIP
Louisiana (LA)	800-334-8626
Maine (ME)	800-533-9595
Maryland (MD)	800-543-1036
Massachusetts (MA)	800-227-6277
Michigan (MI)	800-543-2YES
Minnesota (MN)	800-657-3700
Mississippi (MS)	800-WARMEST
Missouri (MO)	800-877-1234
Montana (MT)	800-541-1447
Nebraska (NE)	800-228-4307
Nevada (NV)	800-NEV-ADA8
New Hampshire (NH)	800-FUN-IN-NH
New Jersey (NJ)	800-JER-SEY7
New Mexico (NM)	800-545-2040

New York (NY)	800-CALL-NYS
North Carolina (NC)	800-VIS-ITNC
North Dakota (ND)	800-HELLO-ND
Ohio (OH)	800-BUC-KEYE
Oklahoma (OK)	800-652-6552
Oregon (OR)	800-547-7842
Pennsylvania (PA)	800-VIS-ITPA
Rhode Island (RI)	800-556-2484
South Carolina (SC)	800-346-3634
South Dakota (SD)	800-S-DAKOTA
Tennessee (TN)	800-GO2TENN
Texas (TX)	800-88-88-TEX
Utah (UT)	800-233-8824
Vermont (VT)	800-VERMONT
Virginia (VA)	800-VISIT-VA
Washington (WA)	800-544-1800
West Virginia (WV)	800-CAL-LWVA
Wisconsin (WI)	800-432-TRIP
Wyoming (WY)	800-225-5996

Cities

Cities of all sizes also have web sites available that promote local sights and events. More sophisticated web sites offer visitors the opportunity to book reservations on-line for hotels, plays, sporting events, and more! However, it can be a challenge to find the "official" city web site. To save time, visit a web site like www.citysearch.com, www.digitalcity.com, or www.4cities.com, where you simply type in the name of the city you are interested in to reach the appropriate site. For additional information, state tourism offices should be able to provide you with a phone number for the chamber of commerce in the city you plan to visit.

We learned the importance of researching local events on a visit to Washington, D.C. Unbeknownst to us, police had cordoned off the area around the capitol because of a rally. Our family ended up walking several miles to reach a museum that was only a few blocks from our parking spot. Thankfully the rally was over by the time we walked back to our car!

Parks

State and national parks offer outdoor entertainment from historical sites to natural wonders. You can obtain state park information either from the state's web site or its toll-free tourism number. Learn more about the 379 parks maintained by the National Parks Service at their official web site, www.nps.gov. Information on national parks is also available by phone from the National Parks Service Public Inquiries Office at (202) 208-4747.

Theme Park Trips

At some point, most families make a pilgrimage to one of our country's enormous theme parks. Quite honestly, our trip to Disney World in Orlando, Florida, ranks as one of the best all-around vacation trips our family has taken. Park designers wisely insure that there is truly "something for everyone." Still, families who want the youngest member of the family to really enjoy the experience may choose to wait until he or she is at least three years of age. In planning your trip, you will have many opportunities to balance convenience and cost. Staying on-site is more expensive but offers easier access to park transportation, early-entry passes, extended park hours, and other perks that reduce "line time."

There is a reason why theme park vacations are some of the most well-documented, with numerous excellent "guide" books available (we used *The Unofficial Guide to Walt Disney World*). Few trips benefit from microplanning as much as theme park trips do—from which rides are appropriate for different ages to what parts of the parks are least crowded at various times of day. Minimize your wait in lines by making as many reservations by phone as possible for meals and for shows. Be aware that opening and closing times and the scheduling of special events change frequently. Verify *everything* when you arrive at the park.

Choose Your Transportation

To some extent, your choice of vacation type and destination will dictate the mode of transportation. In today's fast-paced society, many families want to get where they want to be as quickly as possible; in other words, by plane. Conversely, sometimes "there and back" may be an integral part of your vacation, which would indicate travel by car or train.

The number of different sights you plan to visit will also impact the transportation you choose. Moving from one activity to another each day usually requires a car. Whether you bring your own or rent one once you're there is dependent on your budget. Our family usually drives, for several reasons. It's economical. Driving allows us the greatest degree of flexibility. And with a family of five, we are most comfortable in our own van. Depending on the size of your vehicle and the number of miles on its odometer, you may consider renting a "ride" for a long road trip.

PLAN MODESTLY

The biggest travel mistake most families make is planning to do too much. Parents sometimes forget that *everything* takes longer with children, including travel (their legs are shorter, for one thing!). Keeping daily goals modest allows time for rest or to linger at points of interest. Then there are those inevitable delays that crop up during any trip: road construction, mechanical difficulties, and potty breaks. Consciously building free time into your schedule will give your vacation a more relaxing, unhurried tone.

When traveling with kids you won't be able to see or do as much as you could B.C.—before children. But you may still be able to take in some more "adult" sights if your child is old enough to understand the concept of negotiation. Encourage him or her to behave during a couple of hours sightseeing in the morning by promising playtime at the park or pool in the afternoon. Keep everyone's interest and energy level up by interspersing longer busy days with quieter, restful ones.

Most adults don't feel like they've had a vacation without some time to themselves. If at all possible, try to arrange "alone time" for you and your spouse, individually and together. If you will be visiting friends or family, ask them, in advance, if they would be willing to baby-sit or to find a reliable baby-sitter for you. Often family-oriented hotels and resorts offer child care or children's activities that can give you a break. Just be sure to check out the program or sitter carefully before signing up.

TRAVEL OFF-PEAK

Taking a trip during the off-season (when most kids are in school) has obvious advantages. Rates are usually cheaper and crowds are smaller. When all of our children were preschoolers we couldn't wait for September and October to come so we could go on vacation. But traveling off-peak isn't just for families with young children. Between teacher in-service days and Monday holidays, schools often allow kids several minibreaks of three or four days each during the year. Take advantage of these long weekends and avoid the summer crowds.

Chapter 3

Preparing for a Trip

With the majority of the big travel decisions made, it's time to get down to the nitty-gritty details of getting ready to go. Mobilizing a family for a trip can feel like you are preparing an army for maneuvers. In addition to packing all the *stuff*, there are ways to prepare your children for their vacation experience that will make the trip run more smoothly.

Prepare Babies Early

Comfort and consistency are of primary importance to infants and toddlers. Provide continuity for little ones by acquainting them with any new "gear" you plan to use on your trip before you leave.

Unpack the portable crib and begin using it several weeks before your trip. (This also assures that the equipment is in proper working order and that you know how to use it!) Pull out the backpack carrier and let your child ride in it on as many walks and errands as possible the month before you leave. Making your baby comfortable with new equipment in advance will lessen his or her disorientation from travel later.

Both nursing moms and moms using formula may want to consider their baby's feeding habits when preparing for a trip. If you are at all shy about nursing in public, introduce your baby to a bottle (filled with breast milk if you are worried about your milk supply) well in advance of your departure date. Private facilities and opportunities for nursing can be hard to come by in some travel situations. And presenting a baby with a bottle for the first time when you're both desperate is *not* a good idea. For moms using formula that is always warmed up, start giving your baby several bottles of formula a day at room temperature. That way your infant won't skip a meal if the bottle can't be warmed while traveling. Prepare "meals" for the trip in advance by scooping dry formula into bottles and closing tightly. Adding bottled water later makes your carry-ons lighter and reduces spills.

GENERATE EXCITEMENT

When does your vacation start? Often we don't consider ourselves officially "on vacation" until reaching our final destination. However, changing your mind-set to include departure preparations sets a positive tone for the rest of the trip. We prepare our young children by showing them pictures of the people and places they'll be visiting. Familiarizing them ahead of time helps generate excitement about the vacation and decreases their anxiety along the way. We also invite our kids' cooperation in putting away a few of their favorite toys until we leave for the trip. Small children may not understand the concept of travel, but the anticipation of playing with a favorite toy again can spark their interest.

A friend of mine, Cheryl, generates excitement about their family vacations by starting with a game the month before they leave. She and her husband will start by telling their girls, "I know something you don't know!" Everyone's anticipation grows as the children try to guess where they will be going. Stimulate older kids' interest by having them read travel books and brochures or by watching videos about your destination together. Show children on a map where you will be going.

PREPACK

Becoming a good packer takes practice. But whether this is your first trip or your twentieth, you will not do a good job if you leave packing to the night before you go. Try setting out your suitcases a week or more before you leave. I designate a corner of our bedroom as a "staging area" up to a month before a vacation and start stacking things we need to bring as I think of them. If this creates too much clutter for you, at least start a list a month early. Keep a pad of paper somewhere handy to jot down ideas anytime they come to you. Prepacking not only helps you remember everything you need, it also gives you time to thoughtfully pare down what you bring, lightening the load.

CHECK THE WEATHER

Particularly for trips of a week or less, the wealth of information available about weather forecasts allows you to pack specifically for sun, rain, or snow. Virtually every cable TV company offers the Weather Channel as part of its programming. However, if you don't want to sit in front of the TV until the forecast is shown for the area you plan to visit, there are numerous internet sites that offer city-specific weather information. Many of the web sites for states (discussed in Chapter 2) have links to local weather fore-

casts. You can also find weather reports on-line at
www.usatoday.com/weather/wfront.htm.

Or fill in the blanks below with the name of the
state or city you will be visiting for these web sites:

www.weather.com/weather/us/states/_____.html
www.weather.com/weather/us/cities/_____.html

PACKING

What you bring along when you travel determines, to a large extent, whether a trip will be comfortable for your family. There's a delicate balance
between supplying everyone's wants and needs and
not having enough room for your child's favorite
two-foot-tall stuffed dog! Regardless of the type of
trip you will be taking, here are some guidelines for
what things are optional and what not to leave home
without.

If you will be traveling for more than a week,
pack enough clothes for seven to ten days and plan
to wash along the way. Pack clothes and other personal items that can do double duty: a coat with a
zip-out liner for all kinds of weather, plastic sandals
for the pool that double as slippers, one bottle of
shampoo or lotion that everyone can use. Families
who plan to attend crowded amusement parks or
other tourist attractions may want to pack the same
brightly colored hat or shirt for each traveler (in

appropriate sizes) so that family members can be easily located in a large group.

Visitors to metropolitan areas don't need to pack an entire trip's worth of diapers, formula, and snacks. Restock once you arrive. Let any child with an interest in packing help you select which clothes to bring. Kids feel more comfortable in their favorites, which cuts down on whining later. And by discussing clothing options, you'll be teaching them how to pack too!

Whether we're traveling by plane, car, or train, I've found it helpful for each traveler to have a carry-on bag for necessities and entertainment. On the plane or train the rest of our luggage is obviously not easily accessible, but the way suitcases are wedged in the back of our van for a road trip, it's *safer* to have what we need readily at hand on those trips too.

Baby Must-Haves

If you will be carrying a diaper bag, include a couple of extra outfits for your child and an additional blouse for yourself (especially if your infant is prone to spitting up). We've learned to pack two times as many diapers, food, formula, and snacks as we expect to need for that day. Vacationers routinely run into delays that can increase travel time by hours—flight delays due to weather or mechanical problems, driving delays because of road construction and traffic accidents. Either way, you don't want to be stuck without these items! A multipurpose blanket packed in your bag can be used as a warm cover, a sunshade, a changing pad, or a floormat as needed. Bring several large plastic Ziploc bags to contain dirty clothes, dirty diapers, and other messes.

Toddler Take-Alongs

In addition to entertainment, snacks and drinks will be uppermost on your toddler's mind, so pack plenty. Bringing at least one nonspill sippy cup will allow for refills when needed. Parents with a child who is potty training may want to bring along a portable potty seat, or even an actual potty if traveling by car. (Our potty chair has saved us at many roadside stops!) Whether your child uses a potty chair or not, packing a large, heavy-duty plastic trash bag can save a mattress in the event of a nocturnal "accident."

Mom's Bag

If you aren't toting a diaper bag (or even if you are), consider putting your "carry on" items, including things that normally go in a purse, into a backpack to leave your hands free. Include items to handle minor "emergencies," like a small sewing kit, individual packets of tissues and damp wipes, a stain-remover stick or wipes, a lightweight camera, sunscreen, and batteries. Don't bother packing much in the way of entertainment for *you* unless your kids are older. Finally, try not to overfill Mom's bag, as you will inevitably be asked to carry something of someone else's.

PREPARE FOR ILLNESS OR INJURY

Families, particularly those traveling with young children, should be wary of contact with others who are sick for at least two weeks before a trip. If you are concerned about the health of a family member, go to the doctor before you leave. This is not the time for a "wait and see" attitude! Pack medical information, including your insurance card and physician's phone number, where it will always be with you and easily accessible.

Hopefully you have developed a relationship of trust with your doctor that will permit a phone call while on a trip to request medication based on your observations. However, for those times you are unsure about the cause of illness or pain, find out the location of the nearest clinic or emergency room as soon as you arrive at a destination. If you do have to visit a medical office on vacation, remember that the practitioner will not have access to your child's medical history and will know nothing of your parenting ability. Be prepared to answer lots of questions.

On a Caribbean cruise with her husband and two preschoolers, my friend Dove found that the most important things to have on hand in case of illness were cash and her "papers" (driver's license, visa, passport). "My son became ill on our trip. When we reached an island port, things had gotten serious enough that he needed to see a doctor. The ship's physician had gone ashore and could not be found. So after a couple of hours, I asked to see a doctor on the island. Personnel from the cruise ship did a wonderful job of shuttling us to the office and expediting our appointment. Afterward the doctor said, 'Now there's the matter of my fee.' It didn't occur to me that my insurance card would be useless. Thank goodness U.S. dollars do wonders! However, by the time we were finished, we almost didn't make it back. If you aren't on board the ship when it leaves, the cruise line will fly you back to your original departure point, but you will need your papers, and more money until you can rejoin the rest of your family. My advice is use the doctor on the ship!"

Bring along a small medical kit for everyday ailments with the following:

- any prescribed medications for family members
- acetaminophen in an appropriate strength for each traveler
- antibiotic ointment and bandages

- decongestant-antihistamine medication
- thermometer
- medicine for motion sickness

SAFETY IN A CROWD

Being separated in a crowd is every parent's nightmare. Before you travel, train your child not to run away from you and to always stay within your sight. Tell him to yell out your full name (not "mommy") while standing in the same spot if he can't find you. As you travel, show your child how to identify people who can help him if you become separated: police officers, security guards, store clerks, and other moms.

Keep track of young children by corralling them in a stroller or wagon. Remind kids not to wander off with any stranger, even if they promise candy or gifts, and just in case, always carry current photos of your kids with you.

LET IT ROLL

For children old enough to keep track of their own luggage, a suitcase with wheels introduces them to one of the responsibilities of travel. They can proudly tote their own belongings! We've found that smaller individual suitcases work wonderfully on short trips. But for longer vacations, we still pack one large suitcase (on wheels) for our three children's clothing. This economizes on space and allows the kids to concentrate on their individual carry-ons.

BEFORE LEAVING HOME

To insure your homecoming is a happy one, run through this checklist before you head out the door.

- Put valuables like jewelry and important papers in a safety deposit box.
- Unplug appliances and adjust the thermostat.
- Run the garbage disposal and the dishwasher. Open the door on the dishwasher and washing machine if the insides are damp to prevent mildew.
- Clean all perishables out of the refrigerator.
- Arrange for a neighbor to pick up your mail and paper if you haven't temporarily stopped service.
- Let someone know your itinerary and the phone numbers where you will be staying.
- Make sure all doors and windows are closed and locked and that you have all tickets, confirmations, and directions.

CHAPTER 4

Stopping for the Night

THINKING BACK ON THE HOTELS we stayed in when I was a child, I remember vividly beds that vibrated by virtue of coin-fed "magic fingers" machines and bath towels with the hotel name printed on them hanging in green-tiled bathroooms. Overnight accommodations have changed a lot since then! Today you may not be able to enjoy "magic fingers," but many hotels allow kids to stay free, offer a continental breakfast at no charge, and have the Disney Channel on cable TV.

CONSIDER YOUR OPTIONS

Options abound for places to spend the night. However, with kids in tow, not all accommodations are equal. Before calling hotels, make a list of the amenities you want. We want our kids to be able to burn off some energy at the end of a day of traveling, so we try to stay at a hotel with a pool or playground. If these "extras" aren't available on-site, something nearby may suffice.

One year I was driving back to Illinois from Texas with my mother (who doesn't swim) and three nonswimming preschoolers. Obviously a dip in the hotel pool was not an option, but I wanted to preserve the novelty of visiting a fast-food restaurant with a playground as a treat while driving the next day. Instead, I made a reservation in a hotel directly across from a large shopping mall. That evening we all headed over for dinner at the mall cafeteria followed by a long walk inside.

GET IN TOUCH

Since getting an adequate amount of rest is especially important when traveling with children, it pays to shop around for the most comfortable, affordable accommodations for your family. For this purpose, hotel information on the internet is a good place to start, but not as complete or reliable as calling by phone. Web sites for major hotel chains do provide information about location and amenities. Most sites also offer the ability to compare rates, check room availability for the date of your stay, and reserve a room. It's often difficult, however, to pinpoint your particular rate. For instance, you may be able to check only the rate for two adults in a room.

Once you've located hotels in which you have an interest, it pays to contact them by phone to compare rates and make a reservation. On a recent trip to Chicago, we managed to make a reservation at the hotel of our choice (even though it was full according to the web site) and at a forty-dollar-per-night savings over the stated rate (thanks to a special promotion *not* noted on the internet).

HOTEL CONNECTIONS

www.marriott.com

Marriott Hotels, Resorts, Suites	800-228-9290
Courtyard	800-321-2211
Residence Inn	800-331-3131

www.embassysuites.com

Embassy Suites	800-362-2779
Hilton	800-445-8667
Doubletree	800-424-2900
Hampton Inns	800-426-7866

www.basshotels.com/holiday-inn

Holiday Inn	800-465-4329

www.ramada.com

Ramada Inns	800-272-6232

www.bestwestern.com
Best Western   800-528-1234

www.hyatt.com
Hyatt   800-223-1234

www.sheraton.com
Sheraton   800-325-3535
Westin Hotels   800-228-3000

www.radisson.com
Radisson Hotel   800-333-3333

www.hotelchoice.com   800-424-6423
Comfort Inn, Suites
Quality Inns
Sleep Inn
Rodeway Inns
Econo Lodge

Many travelers think of companies like AAA as
providing only roadside assistance, but they also provide a number of excellent travel services. Members
can request free maps and travel guides for the area
they plan to visit. The travel guides include information on attractions and sites of interest, restaurant
descriptions and ratings, and are another good ref-
erence for hotel accommodations (listed by state and
city). If a number for AAA is not listed in your local
phone book, the office nearest you can be reached
by dialing 800-AAA-HELP.

SUITES FOR LARGER FAMILIES

One thing that's readily apparent to vacationing families is that the world of travel is *not* geared to groups larger than four. Traditional hotel rooms rarely hold more than two double beds. Even at Walt Disney World families are not allowed more than four to a room (except in rare cases). We have five members in our family, and it does feel like a struggle sometimes to fit our round peg of five into the travel square of four.

While most hotels offer roll-away beds, that additional piece of furniture combined with all the luggage can result in a cramped and uncomfortable stay. In an interesting twist, the proliferation of business travelers on extended stays has actually provided larger families with better accommodations, thanks to the many "all suite" hotels or inns now available. Suites have more bed space (usually in the form of an additional fold-out couch or loveseat) and a kitchenette, which cuts down on expensive meals out. Be sure children understand that any minibar items provided in a hotel refrigerator are off-limits, or you will have an unpleasant surprise on your bill at checkout.

Some traditional hotel chains also offer a few "suites" or "family rooms" (a two-room setup where one double bed is actually in a room by itself, with a door that closes between the two). The other two double beds and bathroom are in an adjoining room. If your children are old enough to watch some TV on their own, the "family room" allows adults some quiet time to decompress.

STAY IN A PARK

To add a little adventure to your trip, consider staying in one of the cabins or lodges located in a state or national park. These accommodations are usually clean and tidy, and reasonably priced. The kids probably won't be able to watch cable TV, but recreational activities like hiking, swimming, biking, and boating are often close by.

In fact, for our kids the highlights of our family vacations the past few years have been the parks where we stayed. Last summer, on a recommendation from an Arkansas native, we visited Petit Jean State Park in Arkansas. We stayed in a spacious four-room cabin (including a full kitchen) originally built by the Civilian Conservation Corps. The park had two swimming pools, a large playground, numerous hiking trails to view a beautiful waterfall, and a naturalist program that culminated in a large campfire.

Should your travel plans land you near a park of interest, take a chance on their accommodations. But make your reservations as early as possible. Some parks reserve lodging space from six months to one year in advance! Contact information for state parks is usually available on each state's web site or from their 1-800 phone numbers (all listed in Chapter 2, "Planning Ahead"). Find out about lodging in National Parks from the web site www.nps.gov or by phone at (202) 208-4747.

QUESTIONS TO ASK

In addition to the number of beds in the room, there are several questions you should ask when making a reservation. The first has to do with cost. If you belong to a travel club or another service that offers discounts on lodging, be sure to ask for that rate. You may also inquire if, by arriving or leaving on a different day (for an extended stay), you can lower your cost. At many hotels kids stay free, but check on age limits as they vary from twelve years to eighteen years of age.

When researching the hotel's amenities, reserve a roll-away bed or crib if you need one and ask about the extra charge. Particularly during busy travel seasons these extras are in high demand and may not be available the day you arrive. See if the hotel offers a meal plan. The most common of these is a free "serve your own" continental breakfast, which can range from hot pancakes and sausage to cold cereal and donuts. Ask for a room on the ground level so you won't have to carry luggage and kids up and down stairs. Finally, those preferring a smoke-free room should request one when making a reservation.

CHAPTER 5

Arranging Your Home Away from Home

PART OF THE ALLURE of travel is the chance to spend the night somewhere different. However, depending on your child's age and temperament, a night away can either be a great adventure or a scary excursion. When we arrive at our overnight accommodations, the first thing everyone does is lay claim to their own personal space. Like discoverers in a new world, each child stakes out a bed (or at least a "side" of a bed) and designates a place for his or her "stuff." Unfortunately, kids' choices, based solely on personal preferences, may not result in optimal arrangements for the family as a whole. With your input, there are ways to arrange your accommodations to make everyone as comfortable as possible, whether you are staying in a hotel, a rented condo, or a relative's home.

STAY SAFE

Often a child's common sense has not caught up with his level of inquisitiveness, so safety should be a primary concern. Moms with young children may want to bring along some of their own safety paraphernalia, like electrical outlet covers or a rubber bath mat, if they will be staying in one place for a while. As with childproofing your own home, the most effective method is to get down to their level. Watch out for corners on furniture and heavy objects like TVs on unsteady stands. Put breakable items and cleaning supplies up out of reach and tuck away dangling electrical or window-covering cords.

Kids seem even more likely to come up with ways to injure themselves—oftentimes ways completely beyond a mom's forethought—on a trip than at home. Our only injury-related trip to the emergency room resulted from our youngest tripping and hitting his eyebrow on a metal bed frame while at the beach one summer. That accident demonstrated to us that regardless of how we rearranged the environment, vigilance was still necessary to keep our kids safe.

In addition to physical safety, travel introduces families to situations where different levels of care and awareness are required than at home. Having a door that automatically locks when closed may be a novelty to a small child, but is not so exciting when, upon returning with more luggage or a bucket of ice, you find yourself locked out! Growing up in a small town where many people leave their homes unlocked, our kids were dumbfounded as to the purpose of the security peephole installed in hotel doors. Those too short to reach the peephole had to be reminded again and again to ask who was at the door before opening it!

GET COMFORTABLE

Bringing a little piece of home with you on a trip makes any place more comfortable and inviting. To help a young child feel secure, bring along a favorite blanket or stuffed animal. Let her see you pack the "lovey" before you leave so she'll know it's *really* traveling along with you. Come up with a system so you will remember to repack it after each stop. Similarly, a night-light can be less obtrusive than leaving the bathroom light on, and more comforting to kids than total darkness, especially in a strange place.

If you have a larger family that will be staying in two separate rooms, bring an old baby monitor or walkie-talkies to communicate easily and make everyone feel more connected. We've also found that a portable cassette player with story tapes or soft music works better than the TV at helping everyone wind down and fall asleep after a long day of travel.

SLEEPING GEAR

Bringing along your own portable crib has many advantages. First, there's no worrying about the availability of a crib at your destination. Second, your baby is already familiar with the accommodations and may settle down more easily. Finally, portable cribs take up less space in your room than the type a hotel usually provides, and it can double as a playpen at rest stops on the road.

We never bother to carry a side rail for a preschooler who recently graduated from a crib to a "big bed." Instead, place the backs of the chairs that are always in your room against the side of the bed. Don't ignore this precaution if your child is used to a railing. On one trip my son fell out of bed, hitting the corner of the nightstand on the way down. He actually slept through the experience but awoke with a nasty bruise on his cheek that engendered many questioning looks from other adults the next day.

On several trips where sleeping arrangements were uncertain, we brought along an air mattress and portable electric pump. This "bed-in-a-box" came in

handy on an unexpected overnight at my grand-
mother's house and quickly settled several arguments
between siblings who didn't like the idea of spending
another night sharing the same mattress. Personal pillows are also good take-alongs for a more comfortable
trip, especially if someone in the family has allergies.
Cover personal pillows with brightly colored pillow-
cases to avoid confusion with hotel pillows.

NIGHTS AWAY

Sometimes, coming up with a comfortable sleeping arrangement requires a little trial and error. For
example, is it better for the kids to share a bed when
necessary or for the adults to split up and sleep one
with a child? We've found this depends a lot upon
your children. Some kids can settle down together,
while others simply get more revved up. You may also
have an "octopus" in the family—a child who moves
so much in his sleep that he seems to have eight arms
and legs! If so, bring along a lightweight sleeping bag
to contain your "octopus" in the bed.

Although our children sleep in a couple of separate rooms at home, in my parents' house they stay
together in one room. That room gets pretty full
with three beds, luggage, and toys, and sometimes
the kids stay awake a little later than usual. But a few
evening giggles are well worth the good night's sleep
we all get because they feel secure being together.

CHAPTER 6

Eating Out on the Road

EATING OUT WITH YOUNG children can be one of your most unpredictable travel experiences. My mother tells this story about my sister, Cheryl, that illustrates the irrationality of a preschooler's dining requirements.

"One morning, in the midst of a long family road trip, we decided to splurge on breakfast in the hotel restaurant. When the waitress came to take our order, Cheryl (who was three years old) began to cry uncontrollably. Our server kindly offered to have the cook make my daughter whatever she wanted for breakfast. But in between sobs, Cheryl declared, 'I want my mommy to make my breakfast!' What's a mother to do? Somehow I resisted the impulse to rush into the kitchen and whip up some pancakes. We eventually talked her into some scrambled eggs with bacon."

The simple act of eating in a restaurant can cause children to behave strangely. On the one hand, kids may try food they would never touch at home. On the other hand, they can refuse a dish that's always been a favorite because it doesn't "look" the same as at home. Whether you have a robust or a finicky eater, anticipating your child's reaction to dining out becomes easier with some advance preparation and practice.

PREDEPARTURE PRACTICE

Exposing kids to a variety of foods at home makes them more adventurous when eating out. Even if your child refuses to deviate from macaroni and cheese or peanut butter and jelly, offer other food choices and gently encourage them to try a taste test. Prepare your family for meals at "sit-down" restaurants by asking kids to sit at the table at home for a period of time after each meal. (The length of time should be reasonable given their age and maturity level.) Take the time to go over basic table manners together, and practice them consistently yourself. Finally, before you travel, eat a few meals at restaurants near your home to work on additional rules like "no blowing bubbles in your drink with a straw."

FAST-FOOD VERSUS SIT-DOWN RESTAURANTS

Fast-food establishments with playscapes offer oases for traveling families with kids who need to burn off some energy. For us, the opportunity to turn our children loose for a while provides a sufficient inducement to overlook the quality of the food, at least on occasion. If activity isn't an issue and you're looking for novelty instead, try a drive-in restaurant where the food is brought to a tray hanging on your window. However, even the biggest junk food junkie among us gets tired of hamburgers and fries. Toward the end of our last trip, my oldest son said, "I can't wait to get home so you can cook again, Mom." Imagine that!

Alternating fast food with sit-down meals greatly improves the quality of your diet. Choosing a "family-style" restaurant usually ensures the menu will have something your children will like too. But ask to see a menu before you are seated to check food selection and price.

Restaurants designed around a theme, like an aquarium, rain forest, or railroad cars, offer free entertainment for young diners. However, it's not necessary to get too exotic. Our kids love eating at Mexican food restaurants as long as we sit near the tortilla-making area so they can watch.

HANDLING THE WAIT

The biggest challenge to dining out is the potential wait, first to get a seat, then to get your food. When there's a line to be seated, ask the host or hostess to call for you outdoors. The kids can play on the sidewalk until your name is called. Request a booth instead of a table with chairs to allow preschoolers more freedom of movement without disturbing the other patrons. Also try to get a seat with a view—out of a window, that is. Pointing out interesting sites, or even cars in the parking lot, is a good distraction while waiting for your meal.

Travelers with young children should carry in their own entertainment. Toys like miniature cars, plastic animals, or a small box of crayons and some paper will occupy little ones while you order and wait for your meal. For a new activity, bring along a paint-with-water book and a small plastic bag filled with Q-tips. Tear a page out of the book, then let your artist paint by dipping a Q-tip in her water glass and using it as a brush to paint across the page.

If your child is absolutely starving, ask for crackers when ordering the meal. Or stave off a hunger

meltdown—and get your child's daily quota of vegetables!—by visiting the salad bar. Let your child
pick a few of his favorites off your plate.

Baby and Toddler Accessories

A baby may be most comfortable in his familiar
stroller while the rest of the family eats. Ask for an
out-of-the-way table so you'll have room to park
the stroller next to your chair. Moms who are well-
coordinated can even scoot the stroller back and
forth with a foot while eating!

Pack a bag with finger foods and a supply of formula or favorite juice for your toddler. It will provide her with a good meal and is much more
cost-effective than ordering something off the children's menu. If you do plan on ordering a "kiddie"
meal, bring in any of your own utensils that make
eating easier for a toddler. Child-size spoons, forks,
and nonspill sippy cups allow a toddler to eat more
easily on his own and with less mess.

Dining Strategies

Part of the fun in visiting someplace new is in
sampling the local cuisine. Offer everyone in the
family the chance to try regional specialties by ordering at least one sampler platter to share. At a restaurant in New Orleans we passed around small portions

of shrimp creole, chicken jambalaya, and crawfish etouffee. In addition to broadening our culinary horizons, we discovered one new dish for each child to order the next time we dined Cajun.

This tactic also works well at more traditional restaurants where a children's menu is not available. Ask for an appetizer sampler and let your youngster make his own food choices from the platter. For those who want a decent meal but can't face the potential for discord at a restaurant, there's always take-out to enjoy as a picnic in your room.

CHAPTER 7

Getting There by Plane

WITH TIME OF THE ESSENCE and your destination far from home, there's no better way to travel than by plane. Of course, you can expect to pay a premium for speed. But once you add up the comparative driving costs like gasoline, overnight accommodations while en route, and wear and tear on your automobile as well as your nerves, flying can be affordable and downright attractive.

When weighing whether airline travel is your most economical option, don't overlook potential hidden costs such as airport parking and shuttle service or car rental once you reach your destination. Advance purchase tickets, while lower priced, often have severe penalties if travel plans must be changed.

And don't forget to wear a suit of titanium armor (figuratively speaking) if traveling with small children to deflect all the stares of disapproval and horror from fellow passengers as you and your children board the plane! Thankfully, if flying still seems to be the way to go, finding a low fare has never been easier.

SELECT A SCHEDULE

Before checking flight availability consider the days and times you want to travel. Being flexible with travel plans can help you get the lowest fare. The best deals may be limited to travel on certain days of the week or particular hours of the day—and this applies to each leg of a round-trip ticket. However, taking a young child's daily schedule into account may be equally important.

The "white noise" experienced by airline passengers is often celebrated for lulling babies to sleep, in which case naptime would be a good time to travel. Unfortunately, regardless of how tired they were, our children have *rarely* slept on a plane. There's always been too much stimulation (including several hours of uninterrupted time with Mom) to rest! If we scheduled a flight over naptime, our children would inevitably arrive doubly tired and cranky. You are the expert on your child, so make your best guess about a schedule based on her needs and temperament and give it a try.

MAKE RESERVATIONS

For those willing to do their research, the internet simplifies travel by offering numerous avenues to locate and book a reasonably priced flight. For a list of airline company web sites go to www.airlines.com. Or try more general travel sites like:

www.expedia.com
www.travelocity.com
www.americanexpress.com
www.trip.com

These web sites have access to almost all the world's airline seating. They also offer toll-free phone numbers for those with questions. Look in the phone book for toll-free numbers for specific airlines, or call toll-free directory assistance at 800-555-1212 if you can't locate the number you need.

In researching availability, "direct" versus "connecting" flights will be the next decision to make. Flights with connections may be less expensive, but with each flight change the chances multiply for weather-related or mechanical delays. Also, sprinting from one gate to another (or one terminal to another) with carry-on baggage and young children in hand is not advisable. If you will be traveling with a connection on a different plane, leave *ample* time between flights to get to your next gate (travel agents suggest an hour or more).

For those living close to more than one airport, fares may vary depending on which airport you use, so be sure to check rates for both locations. If one airport is the hub for a specific airline, its fares may be higher than at another airport nearby because of reduced competition.

Note Restrictions

Always read or inquire about all restrictions on your fare. Tickets usually must be purchased within twenty-four hours of making a reservation, during which time the rate can be adjusted up or down. Check on your ability to change or cancel a flight if needed. Even in the event of illness, you may not get a refund. In fact, most discount tickets are nonrefundable, but the cost may be applied toward the purchase of another ticket on the same carrier. An administrative charge and the difference between the fares for the old and new flights must usually be paid.

E-Ticket Tips

By booking a flight over the internet you may be able to use an "e-ticket," which works like this: Instead of picking up your tickets or receiving them in the mail, simply print out a page off the internet confirming your ticket purchase. On the day of your flight, go to the airport with your confirmation, a photo ID, and a credit card. At a kiosk in the airport you hand over your baggage and complete a computerized check-in *yourself*. (Don't panic; someone should be available to answer questions.)

While e-tickets are not available for all airlines, they do seem to be the wave of the future. Using this service can reduce your wait at the airport, but it's not without problems. On one flight booked with an e-ticket I mistakenly thought I had also requested a seat assignment. Even though I arrived at the airport an hour and a half early, the flight was already overbooked. But for a passenger no-show, I would have been bumped! The lesson: for travelers making airline reservations by *any* means, always call a couple of weeks before your trip to verify your flight and seat assignment.

Order Meals Ahead

Most airlines offer choices for meals if you make a request early. Selections may include low-fat, vegetarian, and kids' meals. The quality of these special requests is often better than normal airline food. I remember one flight during which my husband and I coveted our children's meals of ham and cheese sandwiches, apples, chips, and cookies over our own uninspiring "snacks" of turkey with lettuce on a plain bun. Other kids' meals we've ordered have been hamburgers, hot dogs, and peanut butter and jelly sandwiches.

Mealtime on the plane is a great way to occupy your children's attention for a while, so make it an experience they will enjoy. Bring plenty of your own snacks and drinks for any picky eaters. While the beverage cart is out, ask for an extra bottle of water or can of juice so you'll have something for your child to drink toward the end of the flight when everything is put away.

SEATING CONSIDERATIONS

On a plane, all seats are not created equal. Indeed, in terms of comfort and safety all seating strategies have their pros and cons. Kids under two years of age can sit on the lap of an adult instead of paying for another seat. This certainly reduces travel expenses but may not be the best alternative, especially for children who can get around under their own steam. The safest way for young children to fly is strapped in a car seat approved by the Federal Aviation Administration (check your car seat instructions for approval).

Airlines will not mind a "free" child sitting in an empty seat. If three or more in the family are traveling you can actually increase your chances of having an empty seat between you by reserving both the window and the aisle seats on a row with three seats together. If the plane isn't full, most passengers will forgo the less comfortable middle seat and your little one can ride strapped in for free. (Kids riding in car seats must sit next to the window for safety reasons.) If you decide to try this and want your child strapped into a car seat instead of using just the seat belt, you will need to carry the car seat to the airport gate, where it can be checked if no empty seat is available. You'll need the car seat anyway if you'll be driving at your destination!

Moms often wonder whether bulkhead or regular seats would be more comfortable for their children. Bulkhead seats, those located directly after the divider between first class and coach, do offer more room. But it can be hard to take advantage of this feature since children should remain seated as much as possible in case of turbulence. And while the larger floor area in front of bulkhead seats provides the most comfortable place on the plane to change diapers, there is no under-the-seat storage available, so carry-on items must be stored overhead during takeoff and landing. Armrests cannot be lifted out of the way, which means you need to be a contortionist to position an infant for nursing; also, young children cannot lie down with their head in your lap for a rest. For all these reasons, try to reserve seats somewhere behind that bulkhead row.

Consider whether your child will be frightened by the sight of the ground rushing by before allowing him to sit by the window. Some kids are fascinated by the patterns of plowed fields and the way cars look like bugs, but if your child finds this unsettling the shade can be drawn. Some parents report that simply sitting by the window increases their child's chance of airsickness, so they prefer to put that child in a middle or aisle seat.

CHECK-IN AND BOARDING

Plan to have all family members present and accounted for at check-in. Due to new security measures, many airports *will not* issue a boarding pass for children who do not accompany a parent at check-in. This can result in the unfortunate situation of Mom having a seat on the plane but the kids being bumped because of overbooking. (This actually happened to us last year.)

With children there are two main boarding strategies. The first is to get on the plane early with "those requiring extra assistance." This works well when carrying a baby because you won't have to stand in line as long to get to your seat, and you might actually find room in an overhead bin nearby to store items you won't need in the air. The second strategy is to wait until the very last boarding call to give your preschooler more time to run around before the flight. Make sure you have your boarding passes in hand if you wait until the last call to get on the plane.

In-Flight Earaches

Any adult who has endured an earache can understand why children become so agitated at take-off and landing. The painful, stopped-up feeling is caused by a difference between the air pressure in the cabin and in the middle ear when a plane changes altitude. The condition is usually worse on descent than takeoff. Kids are more susceptible to discomfort than adults because their eustachian tubes are small and easily blocked.

Those with a cold or chronic nasal stuffiness may benefit from a dose of decongestant before flying (consult your physician first). Help equalize a baby's ears by nursing her or giving her a bottle on

the way up and down. Having the baby suck on a
pacifier also works. Older kids can chew gum, suck
on a lollipop, drink something to induce swallowing,
and yawn to clear their ears. Remember that kids
must be hydrated to have saliva to swallow, and that
conditions in the plane are very dry. Offer decaf-
feinated beverages often, even if it means extra trips
to the bathroom. As a last result, hold a child's nose
gently shut and have him swallow or gently blow out
in "puffs" until his ears "pop."

CHAPTER 8

Traveling by Train

THERE'S A CERTAIN ROMANCE to traveling by train; it's reminiscent of bygone days when life was less hurried. Trains afford families the opportunity to enjoy the scenery and each other's company without the hassles of an airport or the stress of driving.

Children have always been fascinated by trains. But adult interest in riding the rails is undergoing a renewal as well. While the United States continues to lag behind Europe in access to an extensive railway system, many people here make use of commuter trains in larger cities on a daily basis. America's long-distance train carrier, Amtrak, also continues to upgrade its facilities and to offer new lines. So if you

want a new travel experience, a train may be the way
to go.

LONG-DISTANCE TRAINS

Amtrak operates several long-distance routes
crisscrossing the country and offers overnight sleeping accommodations, dining cars, and other amenities to travelers.

Why a Train?

The number one reason for a family to take an
overnight train trip is the novelty of the experience.
You'll be traveling as few of us have, with the added
benefit of enjoying some of the scenery yourself. In
addition, sleeping on the train means you won't have
to arrange overnight accommodations or meals as
you would on a long car trip.

A few years ago my travel agent friend, Joan, and
her family used the train to reach a destination not easily accessible by plane or car. Wanting to visit Glacier
Park in a remote corner of Montana, they took an
overnight train from Chicago to a stop at the edge of
the park, and rented a car to drive in from there.

Why Not a Train?

If time is an issue on your vacation, taking an
overnight train will use up more of your time than

a plane, and delays are still possible due to inclement weather or mechanical difficulties. Unfortunately, it can also cost up to twice as much (depending on the level of accommodations) because you are paying for sleeping space and meals. Train stations are not always conveniently located, and of course, the availability of rails restricts the number of routes.

Expect the accommodations you pay for to be small. Although children do not have to remain strapped in a seat, for safety they still should not be allowed to run up and down the aisles. If your kids are too young to enjoy the sights out the window, bring along plenty of your own entertainment. (One family labeled their train trip "boring.")

Accommodations

Accommodations vary based on the route you take. The two long-distance trains with overnight capabilities are the Superliner and the newer Viewliner. Superliners are bi-level cars while Viewliners are single-level sleepers with extra second-tier windows. Each train offers "deluxe" and "standard" bedrooms. Deluxe accommodations have a little more space and a private sink, shower, and toilet. Showers and toilets for a standard bedroom are communal, though located nearby. The maximum designed occupancy for each room is two adults; however, two deluxe rooms can be combined into a suite for four adults.

Superliners also have a "family bedroom" that spans the entire width of the car and holds two adults and two small children. Beds designed for what is termed "small children" are for those under five feet tall. Families occupying family bedrooms must also use the communal shower and restrooms in the hall.

Families on a tight budget can purchase regular coach tickets and actually sleep in their seats. Each seat has head and leg rests and can recline somewhat. To make the trip even more economical, forgo eating in the dining car and bring along a small cooler filled with food and drinks in lieu of one piece of carry-on luggage.

Eating and Extras

Meals on the train are free with tickets for room accommodations. Someone will come to your room after you have boarded the train to make reservations for mealtimes (the dining car is small, so passengers eat on a rotating basis). You are allowed to order anything on the menu, and all food is prepared fresh on the train. Special dietary requirements can be fulfilled by contacting Amtrak before your trip.

Superliner trains have sightseeing/lounge cars with full-length domed windows to view the scenery, a small convenience store with packaged snack food and drinks, and video entertainment. Viewliners offer video and audio equipment in every room.

Luggage restrictions are generous. Each traveler may carry two bags onto the train and check in three more to be stored until arrival.

Getting Tickets

More information on routes, accommodations, and services is available at www.amtrak.com or by calling 800-USA-RAIL. Your travel agent should also be able to help with tickets. (Experienced train travelers suggest asking for overnight accommodations *not* located over the wheels for a quieter ride.) In regard to ticket prices, discounts are available for AAA members. Also, rail fare for kids under age two is free, and children from ages two to fifteen ride for approximately 50 percent of the adult fare. These children's rates apply only to the rail fare portion of a ticket; the cost of a room is *not* affected. Fares may vary with availability and according to day of the week or time of year.

Amtrak offers travelers a satisfaction guarantee. Those dissatisfied with their trip because of the quality of accommodations or service they receive (or even if their trains are not on time) can file a complaint. Cash refunds are not given, but you will receive a travel voucher, good for one year, for a trip of similar cost.

COMMUTER TRAINS

Are you ready to relax and leave driving in a congested metropolitan area to someone else? Commuter trains eliminate the expense of gasoline and parking, along with traffic headaches. Rates may differ according to the traveler's age and the day of travel. For example, trains traveling to Chicago offer lower rates for children and reduced rates for all weekend travelers.

Know Your Route

The most important travel tip for commuter trains is to *know your route*. Signs for a stop or station can be hard to find. And it's not always easy to hear your stop called, or to collect your children and carry-ons quickly enough to get off. On her first round-trip train ride from rural Illinois into Chicago, my friend Lisa and her daughter accidentally got off at the wrong stop on the way back to her car. Since it was early in the evening and the number of trains running had declined, they were forced to wait a long while.

Check your schedule carefully so you know the order and name of stops close to yours. Make a note of the departure time for the last train so you don't get stuck. If you will be driving to a station to catch a commuter train, you'll have the best chance of finding a parking space—and a seat on the train—at stations farther from the city.

Have a Plan

Be sure you know where you will disembark, and have a plan for getting from there to your final destination. If you will be within walking distance, study a map to familiarize yourself with the streets. If you plan to take a cab, make sure you have enough cash for cab fare. And wherever you end up, have a plan for getting back to the train station to go home.

CHAPTER 9

Day Tripping by Car

LIVING IN A RURAL area, with the nearest mall an hour away, we spend a lot of time in the car. Going just about anywhere for us could be considered a day trip. So as a matter of self-preservation I have learned the importance of keeping the Sumner clan safe, secure, and somewhat satisfied during our frequent outings.

BE SAFE

Whenever you get in the car, whether to drive to the corner convenience store or to visit a pick-your-own orchard an hour away, the number one goal is to arrive back home safe and sound. Did you know that three-quarters of all crashes happen within twenty-five miles of home? Children's car seats can reduce the number and severity of injuries sustained in an accident, but only when they are used properly. If you have a question about your car seat, contact the organization Safety Belt Safe USA at 1-800-745-SAFE. They will personally answer questions by phone. You can also visit their web site at www.carseat. org. On their site you can find information about product recalls as well as how to install your car seat correctly.

Help kids take responsibility for their own safety by teaching them to say "seat belt" loudly, to remind you when their car seat isn't buckled. Use travel time on day trips to reinforce personal information that can keep preschoolers safe, such as their full name, parents' names, addresses, and phone numbers. Try singing these vital statistics to a catchy nursery rhyme melody to make them easier to remember. Role-play safety scenarios with your child while driving. Suggest that if you and your child become separated, she should yell out your name instead of the generic "mommy."

BE SECURE

Being prepared for the innumerable problems that can plague any family expedition assures you some level of security and peace of mind when you head out the door. Every car should be equipped with a road emergency kit and a first-aid kit at all times. These kits can be stored in an old duffel or diaper bag or in a plastic crate left in the car. If you expect extreme temperatures, set the container inside the house by the door that leads to your vehicle, and grab it on the way out.

Customize the road emergency kit according to the season of the year. For example, in the winter add a folding shovel, a bag of cat litter or rock salt for traction on icy roads, and enough survival blankets for riders in your vehicle in case you are stranded. Stock the first-aid kit with medications such as acetaminophen and something for stomach upsets, in dosages appropriate for all of your family members.

Road Emergency Kit	*First-Aid Kit*
battery jumper cables	adhesive bandages in all sizes
work gloves	
large screwdriver and pliers	sterile gauze pads
emergency flares	adhesive tape
large flashlight with batteries	small pair of scissors
funnel	tweezers
gallon bottle of water	antibacterial wipes
can and bottle openers	antibiotic ointment
nonperishable snacks (including ready-made formula and jars of baby food)	instant cold pack
	syrup of ipecac

Stock your car with several other necessities for everyone's comfort. Find an out-of-the-way place to stash a box of tissues, a small roll of paper towels, a container of damp wipes, and a few extra diapers if you still need them. Throw in a bottle of sunscreen and a can of bug spray too. These days packing a car phone is a must—it's the one piece of equipment that offers families the most security on the road. But also consider slipping an old camera, or even a disposable one, into the glove box so you'll never miss a fun moment.

MOTION SICKNESS

Lengthy trips may be out of the question if a family member suffers from motion sickness. But there are some strategies to deal with motion sickness for the short-term. First, have the queasy child focus on the horizon. Try to cover or block the window next to him so he cannot see other cars rushing by. Don't allow a child with motion sickness to read books or play handheld games. Finally, keep meals light that day because excessive or greasy food can set off nausea (not eating can have the same effect).

DAY TRIP POSSIBILITIES

A day trip is a vacation without the hassles of luggage and reservations. No matter where you live, there is most likely something interesting to see or do within two hours of home. Check your local newspaper for festivals held in surrounding towns. Pick up a Sunday paper from a nearby city and look through the entertainment section for upcoming events.

You can discover interesting attractions in some of the most unlikely places. An hour from our small farming community, in Rantoul, Illinois, lies the remnants of an old Air Force training facility. The hangars have been converted into an airplane museum that is much more "hands on" than any of the larger airplane museums we've visited. Our kids climbed into a nose section of a B-52 bomber, explored the inside of a cargo plane, and walked down into a missile silo simulator. We certainly never expected to find anyplace so captivating in the middle of corn and soybean fields!

Day trips offer preschoolers the opportunity to "practice" traveling as well as to see something new. Here are some engaging places for young kids to visit.

Construction sites. Enjoy the fresh air while you watch the cranes and dump trucks from a safe distance.

Pet shops and farms. Some working farms have tours where kids can actually feed and pet the animals.

Orchards and farmers' markets. Pick apples or strawberries, buy the week's produce (be sure to bring an easy-to-carry basket for your child).

Sticks and stones. The closest pond or creek can give a child an hour of pleasure just tossing in pebbles. If a footbridge is available, play a game of Pooh Sticks by dropping sticks into the river on one side of the bridge and seeing whose stick comes out first on the other side.

Town parks. A park is a great place for preschoolers to run off excess energy without running into obstacles.

Bakery or pizza shop. Look around for a bakery or pizzeria where your child can watch the food being prepared. Ask the store manager for a short tour and demonstration, and invite a couple of friends to come along.

Day Hikes

Introduce your child to the wonders of nature by taking a day hike. Your attitude plays a big part in everyone's enjoyment of the adventure, so be prepared for the dirt, bugs, and occasional scrape that you may encounter. Many parks and picnic areas have short paths perfect for beginning hikers. Consider the conditions of the trail in choosing what clothes to wear. Long pants are appropriate regardless of the season to ward off bugs and scrapes. A clean change of clothes left in the car for the end of the hike can alleviate any anxiety about the kids playing in the mud or splashing across a small stream.

Pack high-energy snacks and water in a small backpack for breaks along the trail. Depending on the length of the hike, other things you might want to bring include bandanas (good for hot days and doubling as a handkerchief or bandage), a small first-aid kit with adhesive bandages and antibiotic ointment, hand or diaper wipes, insect repellent, and sunscreen. Travel sizes of these items will cut down on bulk and weight in your backpack. Let your child carry a pint-size backpack or fanny pack with some lightweight items inside.

Don't hurry along the trail to a predetermined goal or view. Intentionally take all the time necessary to appreciate nature as you go. Point out items of interest along the trail (animal tracks, unusual lichen, moss, fungi, or a bright green beetle). Multiply the fun by bringing along an adventurous playmate for your child.

KEEP KIDS SATISFIED

Activity bags and boxes are not just for long road trips. We always leave a day-tripping version of such a box under the seat in our van to eliminate having to load up with toys every time we walk out the door. A metal cake pan with a slide-on lid stashes toys and provides a sturdy writing surface. It also allows kids to attach alphabet or animal-shaped magnets to the top for entertainment. Kids will look forward to playing with their special traveling toys if they're kept separate from those at home. But don't forget to rotate the contents of the box every couple of months to pique their interest. Let older kids fill their own activity bags or boxes.

Once your babies have grown into toddlers, leave a small bag in the car with a change of clothes, a few diapers or training pants, one or two small toys, a nonspill sippy cup, and a nonperishable snack. This way everything's packed and easy to grab when you get out of the car. Take advantage of parks and picnic stops on your outings by keeping an easily accessible bag in your vehicle filled with outdoor toys like bubbles, balls (blow-up ones fit well), a Frisbee, sand bucket and shovels, a dump truck, and sidewalk chalk.

CHAPTER 10

Taking a Long Road Trip

A LONG ROAD TRIP is like day tripping except with more of everything—more stuff, more snacks, more stops, more *stress*. Still, vacationing by car affords families the most flexibility for the least cost. Then there are the memories you'll make. In my mind, few trips will ever compare to the three weeks we spent when I was a child discovering the American West by car, from Texas to Montana and back again. (Even though my parents had to continually tell me, "Get your nose out of that book and look at the beautiful scenery.") When you're driving for several days at a stretch, your car becomes your home. With space at a premium, the more you organize that space, the more comfortable you will be.

KIDS' THINGS

While kids' things are the easiest to contain, they are the least likely to remain that way. Make it as simple as possible for children to tidy their space by restricting them to two containers: an under-the-seat box and a backpack. Use the backpack to bring in those favorite or expensive toys you don't want to leave in the car overnight. Don't allow kids to over-pack, as you will probably pick up toys or other souvenirs along the way. Encourage them not to leave the backseat looking like a landfill by giving each seat row its own trash bag.

Back-of-the-seat holders are another way to store toys and books within easy reach, and kids won't have to dig around for the toy they want. To make your own, get a clear plastic shoe organizer (the kind you hang on the back of a closet door) and remove any wire hangers. With yarn or colorful cord tie the organizer to the headrest in front of your child's seat so the organizer is facing her. Your child can even decorate the organizer ahead of time with permanent markers (perhaps while you're packing).

ADULT STUFF

Moms traveling with older children may find time on a drive to enjoy some of their own entertainment, especially if they're not at the wheel. (If your kids are younger, there's always naptime.) I pack an activity bag for myself with a pad of paper and pen, books including guidebooks, and magazines. For my stint as driver I bring my own portable cassette or CD player, headphones, and either books on tape or my favorite music. Then I can listen to something I enjoy while a tape for the kids plays on the car stereo. (For safety's sake, keep the volume down so you can hear road sounds if necessary.)

LUGGAGE

When we pack up our van for a road trip it is so tempting to cram as much gear in the back as possible until our luggage reaches the roof. Then I remind myself that this is a bad idea for two reasons. First, I can't see in back of me, so I am a driving hazard to those in my car as well as everyone we meet on the road. Second, we always bring more home with us than we start with, so it's already a given that the van will be overloaded on the way back. If, like us, you can't seem to get everything in, consider investing in a rooftop carrier so your vehicle's interior will be safer and less cramped.

For those stopping at overnight accommodations along your route, packing a separate overnight bag means you won't have to unload the entire car each time. Our entire family can live for a couple of days out of two small, carefully packed bags that hold a pair of pajamas, toiletries, swimsuits if needed, and a couple of changes of clothes for each family member. Put that bag that holds these items in the car last so it will be the easiest to reach when you stop.

FOOD HANDLING

Eating out every meal gets expensive. It's cheaper, and more refreshing, to eat lunch at a road-side park. Take along a bag packed with nonperishable snacks and picnic supplies. For lunches there's that old standby, peanut butter, and crackers, carrots, or apples. Single-serving cans of tuna fish or chicken also provide protein without needing refrigeration.

Stock a medium-sized cooler with juice boxes, small yogurts, cut-up vegetables, and fruit cups. Instead of filling the cooler with ice and contending with soggy food after it melts, use plastic frozen ice packs. You can also freeze several plastic bottles filled with water or juice before the trip to use as ice packs the first day of travel and then to drink later. (Pour a little liquid out of the bottle before freezing so it won't explode as the liquid expands.) Frozen seedless grapes are a cool treat for summer trips and don't spoil as quickly.

Pulling out a snack usually diffuses, or at least postpones, a whiny outburst. A friend once suggested bringing snacks that take as long to eat as possible. She didn't mean that the snacks should be *hard* to eat, but that they should be smaller foods, preferably eaten one piece at a time. If you've watched how meticulously a toddler works to pick up dry cereal, you know that snack time can take fifteen minutes! So our snack selection includes small crackers, pretzels, and dried fruit. Try not to offer snacks, and especially drinks, until about twenty minutes before a planned stop, so kids can make it to the restroom.

ALTERNATIVES TO POTTY STOPS

Kids have a knack for needing potty breaks at the least opportune moments: when you're stuck in a traffic jam, waiting for a drawbridge or ferry, or after you've just passed the last exit for fifty miles. A friend of mine actually was given a ticket for allowing her preschool child to relieve herself by the side of an empty stretch of highway. There are some space-conscious, if unconventional, alternatives to bringing along a potty seat.

Extend the absorbency of an infant's diaper by double-diapering or by inserting a sanitary napkin inside the diaper. Diapers can still help potty-trained preschoolers too. If unbuckling your child is unfeasible, yet he or she is desperate, pull down their drawers and slide an opened diaper under them to avert an "accident." Bring along a tightly covered container for roadside stops when a toilet isn't available. Obviously boys have the advantage here, as they can "go" into a wide-mouthed bottle (a covered plastic ice-cream tub works well for girls). My friend Sally carries a drinking water bottle with a squeeze top that's filled with a mixture of water and bleach to squirt into a used container. The diluted bleach neutralizes odors until the waste can be flushed and cleans an empty container.

Amusements on the Road

The best way to keep infants and preschoolers happy during long stretches of driving time is by supplying a playmate, which usually means having an older sibling or an adult sitting next to them. Even older kids enjoy the opportunity for one-on-one time with you during a road trip. Whenever you return to the car after a stop for a break or a meal, play musical chairs and have everyone switch seats. Reluctant kids can be tempted back into the car by the lure of a new companion and a new view.

Preschoolers don't understand concepts like time or distance, but they can relate these ideas to the events in their daily schedule. Connecting your arrival time to an activity ("We'll arrive around dinnertime") can cut down on plaintive cries of "When will we be there?" For kids who are a little older, bring along a toy clock. Set it to the time you plan to stop and give them a watch to compare the time.

For extended trips make each child feel special by having them take turns being "king" or "queen" for the day. The royal personage gets to make as many decisions as possible, like choosing where she will sit all day and which restaurants you will visit.

The biggest aid we've found to amuse our kids on a long road trip is a thirteen-inch portable TV with a built-in VCR. We attach this "entertainment center" to the top of an overturned plastic crate with elastic cords and set the whole thing at the entrance to the backseat of our van. All three kids can enjoy screenings of their favorite videos. The TV simply plugs into the van's cigarette lighter, and we store the videos under the plastic crate beneath the TV. Before our youngest became interested in videos, the older kids could watch and quietly listen to videos with headphones while the baby napped. A friend of ours who borrowed our "entertainment center" to drive to Florida reported that her children got a kick out of watching home videos of themselves as babies during their trip.

BACKSEAT BICKERING

With an infant you *have* to stop for feedings and diaper changes (especially if you are nursing). However, stopping frequently to allow everyone the chance to stretch their legs and expend some energy is particularly effective in diffusing a bout of backseat bickering. Get out your bag of outdoor toys discussed in Chapter 9, and play ball or chase bubbles. If the kids start arguing and a rest area is nowhere in sight, try pulling the car safely off to the side of the road and announcing that you will not be moving again until the bickering stops.

As a reward for not bickering, tell kids before your trip that they will earn a sticker for a half day of good behavior. Those with a prearranged number of stickers at your destination will receive a special treat (which must be something meaningful to your child). Another method of positive reinforcement is to hand out some number of popsicle sticks to each child at the beginning of the trip. You can even designate each stick to be worth fifty cents. Every time a child argues he has to turn in a popsicle stick to you. Upon reaching your destination the kids are rewarded based on the number of sticks they still have.

DRIVING STRATEGIES

For families who don't plan to stop for the night, when to leave on a long road trip is a matter of personal preference and of their own internal clock. Early risers may choose to get up *really* early and hope that the kids will sleep through part of the morning (or at least be lethargic enough not to make much of a ruckus). Conversely, night owls may opt to leave in the afternoon and take turns driving all night while (hopefully) the children sleep. My husband and I are of the night owl variety. So when our children were all preschoolers we found it easier to drive the twenty or so hours to Texas in one nonstop trip overnight. It was grueling, but less so we felt than trying to get three very small children settled into a hotel room and then back into the car the next morning. However, it was only my parents' willingness to completely care for our kids on the first day after our arrival so my husband and I could get some sleep that made this strategy workable.

Whether you plan to leave early or late in the day, make it a good start by completing your packing early the night before so that you can rest. We found our kids settled down more easily on an overnight drive if we got them ready for bed by putting on pajamas and pulling out little pillows and sleeping bags to use as bedding. Bring along glow sticks that light up when shaken for kids to play with after dark and to use as a portable night-light. Keep sunshades covering windows next to passengers to help block out lights at gas stations as well as the morning sun.

Now that we take more than a day to make that same drive, we try to intersperse long driving days with shorter ones. We also cover the most miles on that first day in the car when everyone is fresh.

MINIMIZE ROAD DELAYS

Minimize your time in the car with a little research and consideration of your route. There are many resources to help you find your way. In addition to traditional maps and travel atlases, detailed information can be found on the internet. Mapquest (www.mapquest.com) offers printable maps (with zoom-in and zoom-out features), written driving directions, and even a road-trip planner. The famous mapmaker Rand-McNally also offer maps and directions on-line (www.randmcnally.com). If you opt for written driving directions, I would recommend verifying them against a map for accuracy and clarity.

It's not unusual for summer road construction to create delays of thirty minutes or more on a highway *any day of the week*. Road crews often work weekends, and even if they aren't, those annoying orange cones and barrels don't get put away just for Saturday and Sunday. There are two ways to check for construction on your route. The first is to look on the official state web site (as discussed in Chapter 2). You can also check the web site of Rand-McNally. Be aware, however, that the status of any road construction can change literally overnight.

Also give some thought to the time of day you will be traveling through major cities. It's always a good idea to avoid morning and evening rush hours or to use an alternate route during those times.

CHAPTER 11

Camping with Kids

CAMPING, WITH OR WITHOUT children, is one of those polarizing activities—people usually either love it or hate it. If you haven't been camping before don't reject the idea without giving it a try. What other trip can you take with kids where it doesn't really matter how much they run around, how loud they are, or how dirty they get? There's no substitute for time spent outdoors when you need to step back from life's hectic pace and gain perspective.

First decide which type of camping trip best fits your level of comfort with the outdoors, for that in turn determines the kind of gear to bring along. For some adults, tent camping requires a closer proximity to critters, and the ground in general, than they find tolerable. But those families may still enjoy camping in a pop-up tent camper or recreational vehicle. With so many choices available, camping is too large a topic to cover in one chapter. Here are just the basics.

TRY BEFORE YOU BUY

Regardless of your camping style, rent or borrow the type of equipment you would like to use before purchasing your own. You'll have the opportunity to see if your family and camping make a good match, in addition to giving the gear a "test drive." That three-room tent you'd like to buy with all the poles and front door canopy may not be as appealing once you've had to set it up after dark by flashlight!

Make your first overnight a backyard campout, where no one can go inside except to use the bathroom. Next try camping at a site within an hour of home. You'll still be close enough to go back if someone gets sick or the weather turns nasty. At least for the first couple of times, camp with another family who knows the ropes. You'll undoubtedly pick up pointers to use on your own trips.

TENT TIPS

In choosing a tent for your family, remember that the stated occupancy (i.e., two-person, four-person) is a guideline for sleeping space only. To have room for some belongings or to play cards, you'll need a tent designated for one or two people more than your family's size.

Depending on the age of your children, you may want to bring one "adult" tent and another for the kids. Having adolescents stay in an adjacent tent also offers more privacy for parents sleeping in a pop-up camper. Some families also erect a tarp or extra screened-in tent to cover the cooking and eating area in case of rain.

A tent is not a playhouse. Protect your investment by reminding everyone that they should be in the tent only when they are resting, when the weather is bad, or when it's time to retire for the evening. Establish a "no shoes allowed" rule for inside the tent. Bring along two small, washable mats. Set one in front of the door for wiping your feet before you step into the tent. Place the other just inside the door to place shoes on after you come in.

To guard against tumbles and stubbed toes, make tent stakes more visible by covering them with clean, empty cans or plastic bottles. This practice may not be allowed in parks where wildlife (especially bears) tend to harass campers. Ask at the park office about any special restrictions.

CHOOSE A SITE

Before reserving a campsite, drive through the campground with a critical eye. Check each site for size, slope, and condition. Tent campers especially will want flat spaces free of embedded logs or rocks. In case of rain, you should not choose a low site where water runoff will collect.

Think about how close you want to be to a bathroom. Young children who tend to wait until the last minute, or who wake up in the middle of the night and need to go, should be near bathroom facilities. However, camping close to a bathroom usually means more lights, more noise, and possibly more smell.

Consider your children's safety in picking a site. Young children should not be too close to a main road or a body of water. Besides the obvious safety concerns, camping near water may also put you in closer proximity to bugs and other water-loving creatures you'd rather avoid.

CAMPFIRES

Few activities represent outdoor craft better than building a campfire. However, fire and young children do not always mix. Introduce your youngster, in advance, to the concepts of "hot" and "cold" with food at mealtime and water in the bathtub. If you do build a campfire, keep a constant watch to insure your child isn't drawn too close by the beauty of the flames. Some parents use a gated baby "yard" to surround their campfire and report that the heavy duty plastic doesn't melt.

Use this fun activity to teach older kids how to build a campfire. You'll need the following ingredients:

- large pretzel logs to represent fire logs
- small pretzel sticks for kindling
- shredded coconut for tinder
- candy corn for fire
- small marshmallows to represent stones for the fire circle
- small cup full of juice to represent the water bucket

On top of a paper towel or napkin, ask your child to make a "fire circle" with the small marshmallows. Have him set the "water bucket" next to the fire circle. Break a large pretzel into three pieces and lay the pieces inside the fire circle so they form a letter *A*. Next, sprinkle some coconut "tinder" into the middle of the *A*. Lay small pretzel sticks (kindling) up against the horizontal crossbar of the *A*. Sprinkle a little more "tinder" on top, and place some candy corn inside the center of the *A* to signify flames. While your child enjoys his edible fire, discuss general fire safety and how the bucket of water is nearby to help extinguish the fire.

CAMPING SAFETY

As with any new activity, your child will want to explore everything in the campsite from your gear to the environment and its inhabitants. Store any sharp objects like knives, tools, or fishing gear out of reach of small hands. The same thing goes for matches and lighters.

Familiarize everyone with the appearance of poison ivy (leaves tend to look different as the seasons change) and teach your child the warning rhyme, "Leaves of three, let it be!" Remind young children that they should *never* eat any berry or plant unless it is offered by you, even though birds and other animals can eat any colorful berries they find.

Teach your child something about wild animals before you actually meet one. Animals at campsites are notoriously friendly after receiving many a handout. But they are not like house pets and should never be fed by hand or petted. Let your child know that he is more likely to see animals on the trail if he is quiet while hiking.

Give your preschooler a whistle on a piece of elastic to wear around his wrist. Should you become separated, tell him to "hug a tree" (a euphemism for standing in one place) and blow on his whistle until you come and get him. Our family learned the importance of establishing a signal to help find those who are lost by way of this story from my mother's childhood:

"My father was the quintessential outdoorsman. Our family frequently camped in the woods of east Texas, and Dad used these trips to supplement our pantry during lean times by hunting.

"On one trip, a family friend, Mr. Monroe, came along. After the tents were pitched, Dad and Mr. Monroe went out hunting while my sister and I stayed in camp with my mother. Somehow the men got turned around in the woods and became lost. It was already dusk, but they tramped around for a while looking for the way back. Finally, in darkness, they started calling out 'Ho!' at intervals, hoping my mother would call back.

"Now, the place we camped was near a rather large state prison, and escapes were an annual occurrence. So when my mom heard someone yelling 'Ho!' she became afraid and herded us all into the car to spend the night.

"The men finally staggered into camp just before daybreak. When my dad asked my mom why she didn't answer them, she replied, 'Why, I wasn't going to answer some man in the woods yelling 'Ho!''"

PACKING UP

"A box for everything, and everything in its box" is one of our camping maxims. The incredible variety of plastic containers available today makes it easy to pack and store camping gear. Be sure to clearly label your tubs, or purchase clear ones so you can see what's inside.

Put equipment, utensils, and supplies that are used together in the same durable container with a lid. For example, place all pots and pans, cooking and eating utensils, plates and cups, and dish soap and towels in one plastic tub. You can even use the container as a sink to wash the dishes, if necessary.

A fishing tackle box makes a great holder for first-aid supplies (for ideas on first-aid supplies, see Chapter 9). Carry personal items you'll need for the shower in a bucket or cleaning caddy. (You can punch or drill small holes in the bottom for drainage.) Soft, compressible items like clothes, sleeping bags, and pillows fit well in large duffel bags.

WHAT TO BRING

Here is a general list of the items you will want to bring on a campout. Use it as a starting point to make your own customized list based on your family's mode of camping. Garage sales are the most economical places to pick up camp supplies like cookware, plates, utensils, linens, and towels. There's no need to worry about finding matching sets, and things are easily replaced if ruined or broken.

Sleeping bags and pillows (optional: cots or mattress pads)

Bath towels, washcloths, dish towels

Lanterns and flashlights with extra fuel and batteries

Cookstove or small grill with extra fuel or charcoal

Small tool kit

Swiss Army knife

Rope, twine

Cookware and utensils

Plates, cups, silverware

Two coolers (one for beverages, one for food)

Clothes and personal toiletries

Kitchen accessories: timer, grater, can and bottle openers, resealable plastic bags, aluminum foil, pot holders, paper towel, cutting board, vinyl tablecloth, matches or a lighter, dish soap

Bottled water

First-aid kit

Bug spray

FUN EXTRAS

While camping is usually equated with roughing it, you don't have to give up all creature comforts. Packing a few extras can improve the tone of your trip from "ho-hum" to a "great time." If you have the room, bring along a lightweight foldable chair for each camper and citronella candles to ward off insects. Add a star chart to help find the constellations, and you're set for a comfortable evening of stargazing.

Pack skewers or straightened clothes hangers (the unpainted kind) to roast marshmallows on after dinner. Sandwich the roasted marshmallows between part of a chocolate candy bar and two graham crackers for that favorite camp treat, s'mores.

Plant, bird, and animal identification books provide information as well as entertainment. Help young children look things up when you take a hike, or put together an "ecology hunt" list of things for older kids to find on their own. Bring a plastic "nature box" with plastic bags or containers inside to hold collections like pebbles and fallen leaves. But also introduce your child to the motto "Take only pictures; leave only footprints." Teach him to preserve the beauty of God's creation for those who come after.

Preschoolers may need some additional campsite activities. Bring along small riding toys to cruise the campground and to make trips to and from the bathrooms easier. Make the heat of summer camping more bearable with squirt bottles for a water fight. Or pack a small inflatable wading pool that can double as your child's bathtub.

CHAPTER 12

Traveling With Extended Family

My sister, a single professional woman, accompanied my then two children and me on our first trip with someone other than immediate family. It was an eye-opening experience for us both. Things went well until bedtime. The adults ended up with very little sleep as a result of sharing a double bed while being serenaded by a child snoring. The next morning we awoke bleary-eyed and grumpy, while the kids were refreshed and ready to go.

Although I was accustomed to meeting the demands of preschoolers while in a sleep-deprived state, my sister was not. As I watched her struggle to maintain her sense of humor, I realized that our trip might have benefited from a realistic discourse about expectations *before* we left. Even with the lack of sleep, however, my sister's presence on the trip added so much to the trip for each of us.

GROUP BENEFITS

Bringing others with you can enhance any trip, because each traveler brings along his or her own unique insights and expertise. For example, visiting any museum with motorized exhibits is much more interesting with my dad. His broad knowledge of mechanical devices, from airplanes to cars to robots, expands the experience. My sister, a chemical engineer and former teacher, actually made a trip to an oil and gas museum interesting for my kids by explaining the complex exhibits in language they could understand.

Give someone else a chance to share their passion with your family. Is there an aunt or uncle who loves to camp and hike? Does Grandpa like to fish and Grandma enjoy sightseeing? There's nothing wrong with letting your children learn to rely on other adults as they do something new together.

Traveling with relatives can also take some of the burden off you. One mom I know invites her

younger sister on vacations as a companion and occasional baby-sitter for her three girls. Grandparents
often have similar schedules to young children; they
may nap in the afternoon and go to bed early, giving
you some time to slip out on your own. Seniors also
may be eligible for discounts on rooms and other
tickets that save on travel expenses.

FAMILY PITFALLS

If you live in different towns or states, members
of your extended family might spend time with your
children only a couple of times. As a result, they may
not be accustomed to the noise and activity level of
life with kids. Traveling with children can be overwhelming, and all the more so if you aren't used to
each other! After a visit to an antique car museum,
where we spent most of our time chasing the kids
around to make sure they didn't climb in the cars,
my father asked, "When do you get a chance to see
what you're interested in?" Conflicting expectations
can create frustration for all parties.

Particularly when traveling with older relatives,
differing ability levels can cause trouble as well.
When my mother accompanied us on a trip to
Mammoth Cave, I reserved tickets for a cave tour
that the sales agent assured me would be okay for my
three-year-old. I assumed that any tour appropriate

for the youngest member of the group would not tax the rest of us. Unfortunately, it wasn't the distance or the stairs down that bothered my mother, but the pace of the walk itself. To get everyone through on schedule, the tour moved at a rapid pace that left my mother breathless, and all of us frightened for her safety. (Our three-year-old handled the tour just fine.) Now I know that long walks should not be part of my mom's agenda, so the kids and I hike on our own.

MEETING OF THE MINDS

Because of the differing levels of abilities and expectations on a joint trip, prior to leaving it's important to discuss what everyone wants to get out of the trip. Here are some questions to consider:

What is your usual routine?
What kind of food do you like to eat out?
In which kinds of places would you like to stay?
What are you most interested in on this trip?
What do you *not* like doing?

Strive for a balance that meets some of each traveler's needs. Get specific, including a discussion of who will pay for what. The more details you can agree on before you leave, the less room there will be for misunderstandings en route. In making plans be sensitive to the special needs of all travelers. Take the time to *thoroughly* investigate excursions to make sure they aren't too taxing.

Set some ground rules about discipline before departing, including who will administer it and under what circumstances. Most experts agree that there's no harm in allowing other family members to pamper your kids as long as the situation is temporary. Explain to the adults ahead of time which rules matter the most and where you are willing to be flexible.

A GOOD TIME FOR ALL

As with any trip, everyone is fresher in the morning. So plan the busiest, most taxing activities early in the day. To avoid burnout, build time off from each other into the schedule. When my parents met us for a five-day vacation at Disney World, we blocked out one full day in the middle of the trip for them to explore the international village at Epcot on their own. With that break they were ready for rides with the kids during the remainder of the vacation.

Spending some time apart also helps any time tensions begin to mount. Flexibility can be the key to everyone having a good time.

CHAPTER 13

Entertaining the Troops

"WHEN WILL WE BE THERE?" It's amazing how any trip with any family eventually leads to this one question! Keeping the kids happily occupied while traveling is essential to a mom's sanity as well as a successful trip. In addition to packing a good selection of open-ended toys and activities, it's important to bring a supply of surprises to diffuse tense or bored moments.

If we're embarking on a trip that requires several days of car travel, I start looking weeks in advance to pick up small, inexpensive toys. Each morning our kids climb in the car to find a new little toy on their seat. Looking forward to their "surprise" makes getting everyone back in the car much easier! My friend Dove makes up what she calls "fifty" or "one hundred mile" paper bags before leaving on a road trip. She places snacks, toys, and activities in brown paper bags and doles them out at mileage intervals, depending on how antsy her kids get. Other moms go so far as to wrap up small toys to pull out at crucial moments, like before getting on the plane or when whining begins to escalate.

To minimize the cost of take-along entertainment, ask several other moms to participate in a book and toy swap before vacationing. Each family receives "new" toys to take on a trip, and kids are thrilled to rediscover their "old" playthings upon returning home. Visit your local library before short excursions to borrow books and stories on cassette tapes instead of always buying new.

HOMEMADE ACTIVITIES

It's not necessary to spend a small fortune on toys for a trip. With a few inexpensive supplies these homemade activities can entertain youngsters for hours.

Reusable activity pages. Pull out activity pages from children's magazines and workbooks and have them laminated (or cover with clear contact paper). Bring along wax crayons or dry erase markers and a cloth or paper towels to wipe the page clean. The page can be used over and over again. You can also make up your own activity sheet to laminate with several tic-tac-toe grids and a game of Dots. (To play Dots, first draw a box of one hundred dots spaced slightly apart, ten dots across and ten dots down. Each person connects two dots at a time by drawing a line from one to the other. The idea is to finish a square first and put your mark inside; you get an extra turn when you do. When all the dots are connected, the player with the most boxes wins.)

Traveling felt board. Cover the top of the lid of a shoe box with felt. Fill the inside of the shoe box with felt cutout shapes that match your child's interests or tell a story. If you don't want to cut the shapes out yourself, packages of felt cutouts are available at educational supply stores.

Stories on tape. Record your own voice reading stories for your child. Place the tape in a resealable plastic bag with copies of the books you've recorded. Pop the tape into the car stereo or let your child read along independently with a personal cassette player and headphones.

Pipe cleaner creations. Give kids a bunch of pipe cleaners in a variety of colors and lengths. Encourage them to make letters, jewelry, animals, eyeglasses, or other imaginative shapes.

Edible necklaces. In a plastic bag place a long string of red licorice and a selection of minipretzel twists and fruity cereal *O*'s. Have your child make his own snack by stringing the food onto the licorice. Tie the "necklace" on so that he can nibble pieces off one at a time.

Shape bag. Cut shapes out of cardboard or foam and place them in a drawstring bag or lunch-size paper bag. Ask your child to reach in and deduce what shape she feels before pulling it out. Expand this game while you travel by placing all sorts of small shapes in the bag: keys, crayons, and small toys.

TIME-CONSUMING TOYS

With space at a premium, the toys you pack should be open-ended to engage kids as long as possible. For siblings who are close in age or have similar interests, bring along some identical toys to cut down on bickering.

Infants

Infants are at the same time the easiest age group to entertain and the most difficult. They tend to be lulled to sleep by the motion of travel, but the constraints of staying strapped in a car seat can make them fussy. First and foremost, infants enjoy looking at your face and listening to your voice. For extra stimulation, secure a car clothes-rod across the width of your vehicle (an adjustable shower-curtain rod will also work). Hang toys on plastic links for your infant to look at and bat. Just be sure the links aren't too long. To keep the toys from sliding away when you turn, wrap rubber bands in between the links.

Bring along rattles, stuffed animals, and toys with different textures to hold and chew. From age three months and up, bring as many colorfully illustrated books as you can comfortably pack. Handheld busy boxes entertain and encourage motor skill development, and suction cup toys can sit on airplane trays, restaurant tables, or attached to a car window.

Preschoolers

Preschoolers are more easily distracted but often require constant attention to keep them happy. As with infants, an adult should plan on sitting next to a preschooler for the majority of a trip. Coloring books, blank pads of paper, stencils, and stickers are popular with kids of this age. Trade crayons for a box of colored pencils (don't forget a sharpener) or washable markers. Reusable vinyl stickers can turn a window into a canvas. Classic drawing aids like Magic Slates, Magna Doodle, and Etch-A-Sketch can be used for many activities. Our kids like to draw "maps" to our destination on these toys.

With play telephones kids "talk" to friends and
family far away or strangers in the next car. Small
plastic figures like dolls, animals, or action heroes
provide endless opportunities for new story lines.
Hand or finger puppets also encourage imaginative
play. Preschoolers can turn their seat into a super-
highway with miniature cars and trucks. Easy block
sets like Duplos let kids construct new toys along the
way. Finally, remember to bring books, books, and
more books.

Older Kids

From elementary school age and beyond, kids
will prefer to pack their own activity bags, but you
can make suggestions and bring along surprise toys
based on their interests. Kids this age enjoy handheld electronic games and music or stories on tape
they can listen to on a personal cassette or CD
player. Many classic games like checkers, chess, and
backgammon are available in magnetic, travel-size
versions. Similarly, a deck of cards takes up a minimum of space and provides hours of entertainment.

Get your child involved in the trip by bringing
along an extra map and asking him to navigate. You
can highlight the route with a marker before leaving
to make this easier. Have him prepare everyone in
the car for your next stop by reading travel brochure

or guidebook information out loud. (Stop at the "Welcome Center" each time you enter a new state for visitor information.) Enlist help in chronicling your trip by giving him a personal travel diary and a disposable camera.

GAMES WITH NO PROPS

These simple games need no props and can be done while sitting down. Kids as young as age four can learn to play.

I Spy. Someone starts by saying, "I spy with my little eye something _____," filling in the blank with the color of something they see in the plane, train, or car. Everyone else tries to guess the object. Whoever guesses correctly starts the next round.

Simon Says. One person (not the driver) is "Simon" and tells the other travelers to do tasks like "Simon says point to your nose" or "Reach down and touch your feet." Participants should follow only instructions that begin with "Simon says." Doing a task without "Simon says" eliminates you from the game. The last person still playing starts the next round.

Rock, Paper, Scissors. Players start with their hands in a fist and chant "Rock, paper, scissors." After saying "scissors" they either make a rock by keeping the fist, paper by holding their hand out flat with fingers extended, or a pair of scissors by holding out their index and middle fingers. Scissors beats paper because it cuts paper. Paper wins over rock because it can wrap it up. And rock beats scissors because it makes them blunt.

Thumb wrestling. Two players sit next to each other and hook the four fingers of their right hands together with right thumbs standing straight up. The object is to pin down your opponent's right thumb using your right thumb and nothing else.

Quiet Game. Everyone agrees to see who can be the quietest the longest. You can impose a maximum amount of time or mileage to give the kids a limit to shoot for.

Guess My Number. Someone thinks of a number between one and ten, twenty, or one hundred (depending on the age of the players). The other players try to guess the number by asking yes or no questions like, "Is the number bigger than five?" Everyone takes a turn with a guess and more numbers are eliminated. Whoever figures out the number wins and starts the next round.

Opposites. This is a wonderful way to introduce preschoolers to the concept of opposites, and to increase the vocabulary of older travelers. Someone calls out an adjective or adverb. The next person responds with the opposite, and then offers a new adjective or adverb. (Examples: sweet-sour, hot-cold, quickly-slowly, imaginary-real, wrinkled-smooth, purposefully-aimlessly)

Finish the Story. Someone starts telling a story, stopping at a crucial point. The next player continues with his own creative version, and so on, and so on. You might want to tape an especially long story to play back later.

Name That Tune. Take turns humming part of the melody from your child's favorite songs. Whoever guesses the name of the tune hums the next ditty. Take time out to sing each song after the title is discovered.

QUESTIONS AND ANSWERS

Family vacations offer the chance to grow closer. An easy way to reconnect with other family members and pass the time is with a little question and answer session. In addition to learning about each other, questions and answers can teach kids lessons about safety and your family's moral principles. If you aren't sure where to start, Brain Quest question and answer cards are available on a variety of topics (including the Bible) and for different age ranges. A pocket edition of a game called Kid's Choices gives examples of moral dilemmas for your family to consider and discuss together such as: "You are on a long driving trip with your family. Your little sister is 'bugging' you more than usual. You feel like hitting her hard but know you shouldn't. Will you hit her?"

People feel valued when they feel understood. Here are some more questions to help you discover what other family members are thinking and feeling.

> What made you mad, sad, and glad today?
>
> What is your favorite sport, animal, TV show? Why?
>
> What is your favorite dessert? How would you make it?
>
> What place in the world would you most like to visit? What would you do while there?
>
> Where do you think heaven is? What does it look like?
>
> What is your favorite room in our house? Why?
>
> What is the toughest part of being a dad/mom?
>
> What would you do if our house caught on fire while you were in it?
>
> In the movie *Pinocchio*, Jiminy Cricket plays Pinocchio's conscience. What does a conscience do? Do you have one?
>
> What are two questions you would really like to ask God?

TAKE-HOME SOUVENIRS

Many people view the purchase of souvenirs as an integral part of a trip. But when you let everyone loose in a souvenir shop, the dazzling array of "junk" creates a galloping case of the gimmies. Especially with older kids, agree beforehand on an amount they can spend and then let them choose what to buy. For young children, provide fresh entertainment by purchasing a souvenir they can play with on the trip.

A postcard vacation journal is a wonderful souvenir of your travels that you can create en route. Before leaving for vacation, pack a scrapbook, glue stick, and pen. Let older kids place postcards into the scrapbook and write out appropriate captions during travel or down time. Or, for preschoolers, punch holes in some small plastic resealable bags and slip a large binder ring through the holes. At each stop on your trip let your child pick out one or two postcards that remind him of the sights. Slip the postcards in your preschooler's plastic bags to make a flipbook chronicling your travels.

For a family travel diary, designate someone who can write to be the "interviewer" each evening before bed. Let everyone take turns describing their favorite sight or activity of the day while the interviewer records the remembrances.

Make a souvenir for everyday use by having kids choose a T-shirt from their favorite vacation spot. Sew up the bottom and sleeves of the shirt. Then fill the shirt with stuffing and sew the neck closed. Vacation pillows make any spot comfortable to daydream and remember.

Afterword

WE'VE GONE THROUGH ALL the nuts and bolts of planning and executing a trip with kids. And, while these steps are essential, there is one more thing you shouldn't leave home without: a happy and adventurous heart. When my friend Tina and her husband took their eighteen-month-old and three-year-old sons on their first vacation trip their mantra was "Don't forget your sense of humor." In fact, Tina says she started repeating it over and over to her husband as they were pulling out of the driveway!

Regardless of how carefully you've made arrangements, things can, and do, go wrong when you travel. Even on a trip to Walt Disney World (a child's dream vacation) it can rain or be too hot, the lines can be overly long, or your kids can be traumatized by life-size cartoon characters. When faced with the inevitable travel glitch, how you respond determines the tone of everyone's remembrances of that event, and perhaps of the trip as well.

Meeting each challenge positively and prayerfully strengthens a family's sense of unity and provides confidence that, together, you can overcome any obstacle. So pack a smile with your belongings and instill a "can-do" attitude in your heart. Traveling with your kids creates memories you all can enjoy for a lifetime.

Heavenly Father, preserve those who travel. Surround them with your loving care, protect them from every danger, and bring them in safety to their journey's end. Amen.

About This Busy Mom

CYNTHIA W. SUMNER HAS BEEN the contributing editor of MOPS International's *MOMSense* newsletter for the past five years. Her book, *Time Out for Mom ... Ahhh Moments*, was one of the first releases in the Little Books for Busy Moms series. She and her husband, John, have three children and live in rural Illinois. For information about speaking engagements, contact:

MOPS International
1311 S. Clarkson Street
Denver, CO 80210
303-733-5353

MOTHERS OF
M♥PS®
PRESCHOOLERS

MOPS stands for Mothers of Preschoolers, a program designed to encourage mothers with children under school age through relationships and resources. These women come from different backgrounds and lifestyles, yet have similar needs and a shared desire to be the best mothers they can be!

A MOPS group provides a caring, accepting atmosphere for today's mother of preschoolers. Here she has an opportunity to share concerns, explore areas of creativity, and hear instruction that equips her for the responsibilities of family and community. The MOPS group also includes MOPPETS, a loving, learning experience for children.

Approximately 2,700 groups meet in churches throughout the United States, Canada, and 19 other countries, to meet the needs of more than 100,000 women. Many more mothers are encouraged by MOPS resources, including *MOMSense* radio and magazine, MOPS' web site, and publications such as this book.

Find out how MOPS International can help you become part of the MOPS♥to♥Mom Connection.

MOPS International
P.O. Box 102200
Denver, CO 80250-2200
Phone 1-800-929-1287 or 303-733-5353
E-mail: Info@MOPS.org
Web site: http://www.MOPS.org
To learn how to start a MOPS group,
call 1-888-910-MOPS.
For MOPS products call The MOPShop
1-888-545-4040.

MOTHERS OF MVPS PRESCHOOLERS®

...because mothering matters

Little Books for Busy Moms

MARY BETH LAGERBORG general editor
written by BARBARA VOGELGESANG

Softcover 0-310-23997-4

MARY BETH LAGERBORG general editor
written by JANE C. JARRELL

Softcover 0-310-23515-4

MARY BETH LAGERBORG general editor
written by LESLIE PARROTT

Softcover 0-310-23514-6

MARY BETH LAGERBORG general editor
written by CATHY PENSHORN

Softcover 0-310-24178-2

MARY BETH LAGERBORG general editor
written by LEIGH ROLLAR MINTZ

Softcover 0-310-23511-1

MARY BETH LAGERBORG general editor
written by CYNTHIA W. SUMNER

Softcover 0-310-23999-0

MARY BETH LAGERBORG general editor
written by CYNTHIA W. SUMNER

Softcover 0-310-23513-8

MOTHERS OF

MOPS®

PRESCHOOLERS

...because mothering matters

Softcover 0-310-21920-5

What Every Mom Needs

Meet Your Nine Basic Needs (and Be a Better Mom)
Elisa Morgan & Carol Kuykendall

After more than twenty years of research and experience with moms, MOPS has identified your nine basic needs as a mother: significance, identity, growth, intimacy, instruction, help, recreation, perspective, and hope. *What Every Mom Needs* is an invaluable resource for women who long to expand their personal horizons and become better mothers at the same time.

What Every Child Needs

Meet Your Child's Nine Needs for Love
Elisa Morgan & Carol Kuykendall

Softcover 0-310-23271-6

Details in a warm and nurturing style the nine needs of every child: security, affirmation, family, respect, play, guidance, discipline, independence, and hope. Don't miss the great stories, helpful hints, and practical suggestions that will help you recognize and meet these needs in the life of your child.

Softcover 0-310-24299-1

Children Change a Marriage

What Every Couple Needs to Know
Elisa Morgan & Carol Kuyendall

This book helps new parents and soon-to-be parents understand the transition from husband and wife to mom and dad, and helps them establish the foundation for a fulfilling and vital marriage relationship. Formerly titled *When Husband and Wife become Mom and Dad.*

COMING IN OCTOBER 2001

In the Wee Hours

Up-in-the-Nighttime Stories for Mom
Compiled by Mary Beth Lagerborg

Lay-Flat Softcover
0-310-24024-7

These short stories, poems, letters, journal entries, anecdotes, and lullabies, by authors such as Chonda Pierce, Erma Bombeck, Patsy Clairmont, and Elisa Morgan were collected to inspire and encourage moms in the middle of the night.

M♥PS. *resources from* Zonder**kidz**

Little Jesus, Little Me
Written by Doris Rikkers
Illustrated by Dorothy Stott
Board Book 0-310-23205-8

Ages Infant to 2 years

My Busy, Busy Day
Written by Kelly Kim
Photographed by
Bender & Bender Photography, Inc.
Board Book 0-310-23206-6

Morning, Mr. Ted!
Written by Crystal Bowman
Illustrated by Liz Conrad
Board Book 0-310-70060-4

Ages 2–4

See the Country, See the City
Written by Crystal Bowman
Illustrated by Pam Thomson
Hardcover 0-310-23210-4

Boxes, Boxes Everywhere!
Written by Crystal Bowman
Illustrated by Jane Schettle
Board Book 0-310-70062-0

Zachary's Zoo
Written by Mike and Amy Nappa
Illustrated by Lyn Boyer-Nells
Hardcover 0-310-23208-2

Ages 4–6

Mommy, May I Hug the Fishes?
Written by Crystal Bowman
Illustrated by Donna Christensen
Hardcover 0-310-23209-0

Mad Maddie Maxwell
Written by Stacie Maslyn
Illustrated by Jane Schettle
Hardcover 0-310-23207-4

Snug as a Bug?
Written by Amy Imbody
Illustrated by Mike Gordon
Hardcover 0-310-70063-9

Just for Mom! These books include a special "Mom's Moment" insight from MOPS International (Mothers of Preschoolers)—the people who know what mothering and children are all about!

Pick up a copy at your favorite bookstore today!

We want to hear from you. Please send your comments about this book to us in care of the address below. Thank you.

GRAND RAPIDS, MICHIGAN 49530

www.zondervan.com